THE MOST IMPORTANT THING

I KNOW™ ABOUT THE

SPIRIT OF SPORT

THE MOST IMPORTANT THING

I KNOW™ ABOUT THE

SPIRIT OF SPORT

101 INSPIRING MESSAGES FROM ATHLETES, COACHES, SPORTSWRITERS, AND COMMENTATORS

COMPILED BY LORNE A. ADRAIN

WILLIAM MORROW AND COMPANY, INC.

NEW YORK

Library of Congress Cataloging-in-Publication Data
The most important thing I know about the spirit of sport : 101
    inspiring messages from athletes, coaches, sportswriters, and
    commentators / compiled by Lorne A. Adrain. —1st ed.
        p.   cm.
    ISBN 0-688-16400-5
        1. Sports personnel—Quotations. 2. Sports—Quotations, maxims,
    etc.   I. Adrain, Lorne A.
    GV707.M67   1999
    796—dc21   98-51011
                                                                  CIP

Printed in the United States of America

First Edition

1 2 3 4 5 6 7 8 9 10

BOOK DESIGN BY CHRIS WELCH

www.williammorrow.com

For my children

Ariane, Sam, and Grace

May their lives be blessed with

The Spirit of Sport

And for the athletes of Special Olympics around the world

CONTENTS

INTRODUCTION
CONTRIBUTORS

ACKNOWLEDGMENTS

First, thank you for buying this book. Your purchase will help support the athletes of Special Olympics.

It is always gratifying to me to experience the wonderful things that can be done when people of goodwill come together to do good works. This project has been no exception; it is the product of the generosity, encouragement, and support of many people.

Thanks to all the generous contributors to the book. Their thoughts are the essence of the project and the true spirit of sport.

To my wife, Ann, whose assistance in editing and writing and daily interest made this a joyful project. To my children, Ariane, Sam, and Grace, who keep me thinking about life's gifts. To my family, especially my parents, Lorraine and Allan, whose example has inspired so many things of which I am proud. To my coaches, teammates, mentors, and friends who have shared so generously with me.

Thanks to Betty Kelly of William Morrow and to my editor, Michelle Shinseki, for her infectious belief and commitment and excitement. To Caroline Carney of Book Deals, Inc., who found me and promoted this idea. Her goodwill and good works will build a legend in the book business. To Vince Agliata, my assistant on this project, without whose daily inventiveness and gentle persistence this would not be the wonderful work that it is. To Ted O'Sullivan and my assistant who allowed me the time to work on this and offered constant support and celebration. To Melissa Hood, whose assistance in research and writing of biographies added richness and dimension to the thoughts of the contributors. To my associates, Roy Ballentine and

Dave Sprinkle, who have provided a model of excellence for all that I do.

To all those who helped with the challenging task of finding the world's greatest and securing thoughts from them. Pat Aldrich, Sue Aldrich, all-American Dave Amato, Linda Baumgartner, John Butterfield, David Chaudoir, Janie DeCelles, Frank and Nancy DeCosta, Paul DePace, Jennifer Devitt, Lisa Dimas, Jay Emmett, Stephen Emmett, Claire Evert, Bob Fay, Greg Foster, Barry Frank, Emil Gaspari, Elaine Gouras, Duey Graham, Jim Harrick, Chris Hunken, Julie Iler, Susan Jantzen, Andrea Mead Lawrence, Bobby Lombardo, Chad Lyons, Joe McDevitt, Pamela MacFarlane, Mike McGovern, Anita Martin, Mike Matone, Pat Mills, Katie Naish, Peter O'Reilly, Priscilla O'Reilly, Del Reddy, Gary Roffe, Paul Rossetti, Blaine Sergew, Zelda Spoelstra, Mark Stenning, Cindy Stinger, Bobbie-Jean Taylor, Kimberly Till, Peter Vidmar, Stuart Weir, and Cindy Whittaker.

On a warm October day recently, I sat with my former high school wrestling coach, Larry West, in a small neighborhood place not far from Narragansett Bay. Over twenty-five years ago, this man with the twinkling brown eyes gave me one of the most important gifts I've ever received. Now, all these years later, I sought him out to check my own beliefs against what he saw in the scrawny teenager who wrestled for him for three years and to ask him what he had hoped I would learn back then.

"With you," Coach West told me as the sun set brilliantly behind us, "it was all about confidence. You had the skill, you had the talent, but you were so afraid to fail you couldn't carry through."

He was right. I remembered how losing a match felt like I was letting down everybody—Coach West, my team, the entire school. Once, after a heartbreaking loss, Coach West said, "The only thing you're missing is the belief in yourself." All these years later, I still remember his lessons, especially this one: in sports, and in life, take risks without the fear of failure.

Coach West also told me that as a coach, his greatest challenge was to figure out what each athlete needed and then to help them get it. For the first time, I realized that somehow, amid all the hubbub of coaching an entire team, he had taken the time to figure out what I needed to succeed. He turned an unsure sixteen-year-old into a confident athlete and captain of the team.

As many of us know, sports tests our mind, our body, and our spirit. It prepares and strengthens us for all the challenges in our lives. If

Coach West had not identified a young boy's lack of confidence, if he had not helped to instill belief in myself and a willingness to risk failure, I would not be the parent, the friend, the member of the community that I am today. Without that confidence and courage, I could not have assembled what you are holding in your hand. I may not have believed that I could make a difference. He helped me understand that each of us has a story to tell and something to contribute.

With that belief in my heart, I wrote to leading athletes around the world and asked them to share a thought about leadership, excellence, and the spirit of sport. I knew that their own stories about how they found their way would inspire all of us. In many ways, the thoughts they shared are simple ones, but they are also universal ones. And each is marked by the unique individual who shares it. From bicyclist Greg LeMond, who came back from a near fatal hunting accident to win the Tour de France twice; to Mike Eruzione, the team captain of the 1980 U.S. Olympic hockey team who, during the last few minutes of a tied game against the Soviet Union, scored the winning goal; to Zoe Koplowitz, a woman with multiple sclerosis who managed to finish the Boston Marathon though it took thirty hours and fifty-three minutes; to gymnast Shannon Miller, who at twenty-one years old, has won more Olympic and world championships than any other American gymnast; to Muhammad Ali, sports legend and humanitarian leader. These are just a few of the remarkable athletes whose individual stories and personal thoughts are shared here.

Inspiration comes to us in many ways, every day. Coach West made my early experience with sports one of growth and inspiration. A continuing source of inspiration for my life and my work has been the spirit displayed by the athletes of the Special Olympics. For twenty-five years, I have watched and learned from these extraordinary people. In grateful appreciation of all they have given me, I proudly pledge this book to their support and encouragement. Each Special Olympics athlete takes an oath that captures for me the spirit of sport and, in many ways, the spirit of life. "Let me win," they say, "but if I cannot win, let me be brave in the attempt." That oath, combined with the teamwork, fair play, creativity, respect, and commitment that sports gives all of us, is reflected in these pages. May they inspire you to do great things.

—*Lorne Adrain*
December 1998

THE MOST IMPORTANT THING I KNOW™ ABOUT THE SPIRIT OF SPORT

Ted Turner, environmentalist, civic leader, and owner of the 1995 World Series champions Atlanta Braves baseball team, the Atlanta Hawks basketball team, and the Atlanta Thrashers ice hockey team, seems to have a golden touch. In 1963, Ted took over and revived his late father's failing business in Atlanta. A few years later Ted's talents for reviving failing business were exhibited in his takeover of Atlanta's Channel 17. Within five years the station went national. His skill and business savvy in the entertainment industry led him to found CNN, currently one of the most popular news networks in the world. Ted successfully launched another television venture, TNT, which broadcasts sports in addition to movies. In 1996, he sold his television stations and networks to Time Warner Inc. and became the corporation's vice chairman. In addition to owning three major sports teams, Ted is a superior yachtsman, successfully defending the America's Cup in 1977 and winning national and world sailing titles. He strongly believes in giving to the community, both nationally and internationally, and gives much of his wealth to charitable organizations. Most recently, he donated $1 billion to the United Nations, for use in programs such as UNICEF, disease research, land mine cleanup, and peacekeeping.

How much you give is how you keep score.

TIME WARNER

R.E. Turner
Vice Chairman

How much you give is how you keep score.

Ted Turner

Greg LeMond's participation at the 1989 Tour de France signaled one of the greatest comebacks in sports history. After he was named Junior World Cycling Champion in 1978 and the Amateur World Champion for 1978 and 1979, Greg's domination of the 1986 Tour de France did not come as much of a surprise. However, in 1987, Greg was accidentally shot in a serious hunting accident, which left approximately thirty small lead pellets in the athlete's body. Against overwhelming odds, Greg came back and again won the Tour de France in 1989 and 1990. During Greg's cycling career he won two world championship gold medals, two world championship silver medals, and became the first cyclist from the United States to have won both the Tour de France and the world championship.

The most important decision I ever made in my career was to live my life in sports as honestly and ethically as possible. Never having compromised my values allows me to look back on my life with no regrets and feel satisfaction in what I was able to accomplish.

LANCE ARMSTRONG

Lance Armstrong, two-time Olympian, cancer survivor, and cancer research activist, has cycled competitively since he was a child. In 1995, Lance cemented his place among cycling's elite when he won the internationally acclaimed Tour Du Pont, succeeded by a dramatic stage win in the Tour de France. In 1996, he became the first cyclist to defend his Tour Du Pont title. However, his fortunes took a tragic turn when, in October 1996, he was diagnosed with testicular cancer and had to endure several operations and aggressive chemotherapy treatment. His illness inspired him to establish the Lance Armstrong Foundation to benefit cancer research. In September 1998, Lance shocked the cycling world and completed his international comeback with a remarkable fourth-place finish in the grueling three-week Tour of Spain and a fourth place in the world championships.

Sport is a way of life and life is a sport. The only one keeping score should be you.

GREG LEMOND

The most important decision I ever made in my career was to live my life in sports as honestly and ethically as possible. Never having compromised my values allows me to look back on my life with no regrets and feel satisfaction in what I was able to accomplish

Greg LeMond

Sport is a way of Life.
and
Life is a Sport.
The only one keeping
score should be
YOU....

Lance Armstrong

PAT McCORMICK

In 1948, then unknown swimming legend Pat McCormick just missed qualifying for the Olympic Games. She decided that she was not going to suffer that disappointment again. She trained for the 1952 Helsinki Olympic Games by doing a hundred dives a day, six days a week. In 1952, Pat not only won the springboard event, she also won the platform event, becoming the first woman to sweep both diving golds at a single Olympics. Pat was less than confident when the 1956 Olympic Games loomed ahead. She was twenty-six years old, making her one of the oldest members of the Olympic team. Remarkably, she had also given birth to her first child just eight months earlier. But Pat repeated her performance and took the gold in both diving events. Again she set a record by becoming the first diver in history to sweep golds at two consecutive Olympic events.

The most important thing I know—when you have a *Dream* and you *really* believe YOU WILL FIND A WAY.

KELLY McCORMICK-ROBERTSON

Olympic medalist Kelly McCormick-Robertson has had her eye on an Olympic medal, literally, since she was a little girl. Daughter of Olympic gold medalist Pat McCormick, Kelly made a bet with her mother that someday she would have an Olympic medal of her own. She won that bet, with emphasis, by winning two consecutive Olympic medals, just as her mother had done over thirty years earlier. At the 1984 Olympic Games, Kelly won a silver medal in the springboard diving event and four years later she won a bronze Olympic medal in that same event. Currently, Kelly has retired from competition and is head coach of her own diving team in Washington State. Today Kelly's pride is her family, her husband, Matt, daughters Alex and Isabella, and son Glenn.

No matter how great your achievement, always strive for the goodness within your heart.

PAT McCORMICK ENTERPRISES, INC.

The most important thing I know —

When you have a Dream and you really Believe —
You WILL FIND A WAY

Pat McCormick

no matter how great your achievement, always strive for the goodness within your heart...

_Helga K_____

After she won a gold medal in the 100-meter dash at the 1987 Pan American Games and set a new record for the 100-meter hurdles, expectations were high for Gail Devers's 1988 Olympic competition. However, after her poor Olympic performance and waning health doctors diagnosed Gail with Graves' disease. She had to undergo extensive radiation treatment and her doctors believed that she would have to have both her feet amputated. Fortunately, a change in her medication led to Gail's dramatic recovery and her return to championship racing. Just one year later she won a silver medal in the 100-meter hurdles at the world championships in Tokyo. Encouraged by her success, Gail qualified for the 1992 Olympics and won the 100-meter sprint gold medal. She also placed fifth in the 100-meter hurdle race. One year later, Gail took home the gold medal in both events at the world championships. Returning to the Olympics in 1996, Gail won her second consecutive gold medal in the 100-meter sprint and won a gold medal as a member of the women's 4 × 100-meter relay. Gail spends a good deal of time as a motivational speaker and as an advocate for children and teens.

Keep your dreams alive. Understand to achieve anything requires faith and belief in yourself, vision, hard work, determination, and dedication. Remember all things are possible for those who believe.

Elite **I**nternational **S**ports **M**arketing, Inc.

Keep your dreams alive.
Understand to achieve anything requires:
faith and belief in yourself, vision, hardwork,
determination, and dedication.
Remember all things are possible for
those who believe.

3 x Olympic Gold

Raised in Reston, Virginia, the Detroit Pistons' Grant Hill has proved himself to be an exceptional and refreshingly modest athlete. Grant led Duke University's Blue Devils to two consecutive NCAA titles and received the Henry Iba Award given to the nation's best defensive player. While attending Duke University he also dedicated countless hours to volunteering for the university's literacy program. During his first professional season with the Pistons, Grant received Rookie of the Year honors. In 1996, Grant played with Team USA at the Atlanta Olympic Games and won a gold medal. Off the court, he continues to give back to his community with programs such as the Special Olympics, YWCA Coalition for Homeless Children, and Meals on Wheels.

God's greatest gift to man is life. Man's greatest gift to God is what he does with his life.

As a six-foot-tall twelve-year-old, Lisa Leslie was encouraged to try out for basketball. In middle school she discovered that not only did she enjoy playing but that she had heretofore unknown natural abilities. In 1991, her first year at USC, she was honored as the U.S. basketball Female Athlete of the Year and she was asked to join the USA junior team. While playing with Team USA Lisa helped her teammates earn a 52–0 record. Then, in 1996, Lisa and Team USA won the Olympic gold medal. Currently she is enjoying a successful career with the WNBA as a member of the Los Angeles Sparks. Adhering to a very busy schedule, Lisa also works as a successful fashion model and sports commentator and she volunteers as a spokesperson for Big Brothers and Big Sisters of America.

To be excellent means to be the best. From my experience I've become one of the best because of my belief in God, hard work and discipline. No matter what anyone says about you, if you strive to be the best and focus in on your goals you too will see how hard work pays off.

God's greatest gift to man is life.
Man's greatest gift to god is what
he does with his life.

Grant Hill

To be excellent means to be the best.
From my experience I've become one of the
best because of my belief in God, hard
work and discipline. No matter what
anyone says about you, if you strive to
be the best and focus in on your goals
you too will see how hard work pays off.

*Lisa
Leslie*

As a child, Chris Evert, daughter of tennis pro Jimmy Evert, was encouraged to spend a great deal of time practicing tennis. At the age of eighteen, Chris joined the professional tour, where, between the years 1973 and 1979, she played 125 consecutive matches on clay without a single loss. By 1976, Chris had not only been inducted into the International Tennis Hall of Fame but had become the first female tennis pro to make $1 million in prize money. She was also the first player ever to win 1,000 matches and 157 tournaments, which included two Australian Opens, seven French Opens, three Wimbledon championships, and six U.S. Opens. Chris held her number one ranking for seven years before being defeated in 1981, by Martina Navratilova. Chris Event holds the highest winning percentage in professional women's tennis, .899%. In 1989, while walking off the tennis court for the last time in her professional career, Chris gave a small goodbye wave to her cheering fans while her opponent, Zina Garrison, looked on in tears.

The difference is almost all mental. The top players just hate to lose. I think that's the difference. A champion hates to lose even more than she loves to win.

Chrissie

The difference is almost all mental. The top players just hate to lose. I think that's the difference. A champion hates to lose even more than she loves to win.

Chris Evert

Dan O'Brien, world-class decathlon athlete, was adopted into a family of seven at the age of two. Despite his numerous achievements—an Olympic gold medal and three world championships—Dan has admitted that every competition terrifies him. Clearly, his fear has not affected his performance. He attended the University of Idaho and holds numerous Idaho and Big Sky Conference track-and-field records. He has been the world record holder in the decathlon, the pentathlon, and in the heptathlon. In 1991 and 1993–96, Dan held U.S. Track and Field Championship titles in the decathlon. He won two gold medals in the Goodwill Games decathlon event and a gold medal in the 1996 Olympic Games. *Track and Field News* ranked Dan number one in the world in the decathlon for five consecutive years. Dan looks forward to having a large family someday and adopting children of his own.

The Spirit of Sports!

The spirit of sports gives each of us who participate an opportunity to be creative.

Sports knows no sex, age, race or religion.

Sports gives us all the ability to test ourselves mentally, physically and emotionally in a way no other aspect of life can.

For many of us who struggle with "fitting in" or our identity—sports gives us our first face of confidence. That first bit of confidence can be a gateway to many other great things!

DAN O'BRIEN

Olympic and World Champion Decathlete

The Spirit of Sports!

The spirit of sports gives each of us who participate, an opportunity to be CREATIVE.

Sports KNOWS NO SEX, AGE, RACE or RELIGION

Sports GIVES us ALL the Ability to test ourselves mentally, physically And emotionally. IN A WAY NO other Aspect of life CAN.

For MANY of us who struggle with "Fitting IN" or our Identity - Sports gives us our first taste of CONFIDENCE. THAT first bit of CONFIDENCE CAN be A GATEWAY to MANY other great things!

Dan O'Brien

JIM RYUN

Congressman, Olympian, and philanthropist, Jim Ryun is one of the fastest runners in history. Not only was he the first high school boy to break the four-minute-mile record, since 1965, Jim's national high school mile record of 3:55.3 has not been beaten. After graduating from high school and going to the University of Kansas, Jim set a world record in the 880-yard dash, the 1,500-meter, and in the mile. In 1967 he set a world-record mile time of 3:51.1 which was undefeated for nine years. Currently, Ryun holds the second district congressional seat representing his native Kansas. He also works as founder and president of Jim Ryun Sports, Inc., a public relations firm that does product marketing and promotes numerous charities.

The Lord Jesus Christ has not called me to be successful as much as He has called me to be faithful to Him and His principles.

LINDA MASTANDREA

World champion athlete, lawyer, and community leader Linda Mastandrea does not let cerebral palsy hamper her life. Competing in wheelchair sports for fifteen years, Linda has been awarded numerous honors including the International Olympic Committee's President's Disabled Athlete Award and was named the YWCA's Outstanding Woman Leader of 1995. While attending law school in Chicago, Linda competed on the U.S. paralympic team and on the U.S. world championship team. After graduation, she went on to compete on the U.S. paralympic team, the U.S. Pan American team, and another U.S. world championship team. Linda is vice president of the U.S. Cerebral Palsy Athletic Association and a five-time national and international record holder.

What I've learned in my years as a competitive wheelchair athlete is this—what separates a winner from the rest of the pack is not raw talent or physical ability; instead, it is the drive and dedication to work hard every single day, and the heart to go after your dream, no matter how unattainable others think it is.

Jim Ryun
2nd District, Kansas

House of Representatives

The Lord Jesus Christ has not
called me to be successful as much as He
has called me to be faithful to Him
and to His principles.

Go with God!

Jim Ryun   John 3:16

LINDA MASTANDREA

Attorney at Law

What I've learned in my years
as a competitive wheelchair athlete is
this -- what separates a winner
from the rest of the pack is not
raw talent or physical ability; instead,
it is the drive and dedication to
work hard every single day, and
the heart to go after your dream,
no matter how unattainable others
think it is.

Linda
Mastandrea
'96 Paralympic
gold medalist
200m

Tara VanDerveer has coached Stanford women's basketball for over twelve years, accumulating a record of five Final Four appearances and two NCAA titles. Tara started her impressive array of honors and awards as a starting guard at Indiana University, where she was named to the IU Hall of Fame. As head coach of Ohio State's women's basketball team Tara led the Buckeyes to four Big Ten championships and was twice named Big Ten Coach of the Year. Tara then branched out into international coaching. VanDerveer served as head coach for six previous USA basketball teams before being named the 1995–96 national team head coach and the 1996 U.S. Olympic team head coach. At the 1996 Olympic Games, Tara and her players won a gold medal. She was honored with both the USA Basketball National Coach of the Year Award and the U.S. Olympic Committee Elite Basketball Coach of the Year.

Excellence is doing your best all the time.

University of Tennessee women's basketball coach Pat Summitt expects a lot from her players, but the rewards are worth it. Pat's teams regularly play in national tournaments and have won numerous NCAA championship titles. Her coaching statistics, a winning average of .808, places Pat second in victories among playing coaches and fifth among all coaches in the history of men's and women's basketball. Setting a new precedent for excellence, Pat coached the 1984 Olympic team that was the first American team to win a gold medal in basketball. Pat herself played for the U.S. Olympic team that won a silver medal in 1976, the first time in history women's basketball was played at the Olympics. Pat's teams have played in the NCAA Final Four games over a dozen times.

Attitude is a choice. Think positive thoughts daily. Believe in yourself!

Excellence is doing
your best all the time.

Tara VanDerveer

TENNESSEE
Lady Vols

Attitude is a choice. THINK
positive thoughts daily. Believe
in yourself!

Pat Summitt

Steve Young is best known as the starting quarterback for the San Francisco 49ers. His outstanding professional football career has lasted over a decade and is still going strong. Young's claims to fame on the gridiron include the honor of being the highest-rated quarterback in NFL history, winning Most Valuable Player in Super Bowl XXIX and in the NFL, and being repeat pro bowl performances.

He set collegiate records at Brigham Young University, which was founded by his great-great-great-grandfather. Steve received both his undergraduate and law degree there. While in school he was the starting quarterback and the leading NCAA Division I quarterback. After graduation Steve played for the Los Angeles Express and the Tampa Bay Buccaneers. He played backup to quarterback Joe Montana from 1987 until 1991, when he was given the opportunity to start. Steve went on to lead the 49ers to two Super Bowl championships, in 1992 and 1994. Finally given his time in the spotlight, Steve proved to be a huge asset to the 49ers and was named the NFL's Player of the Year in 1992 and 1994. He also spends time working with the Forever Young Foundation, an organization he founded and chairs to raise funds for youth organizations in San Francisco, Arizona, and Utah. He is a board member of the American Indian Services and frequently donates his time to youth groups across the country as a motivational speaker. He is also the author of a children's book entitled *Forever Young.*

Being active in sports has taught me all of life's most important lessons.

J. STEVEN YOUNG

Being active in sports has taught me all of life's most important lessons.

MILT CAMPBELL

Milt Campbell is one of the greatest and most versatile all-around athletes in history. In high school, he was the national hurdles champion, a national all-American swimmer, the national decathlon champion, and an all-state fullback on the football team. At the 1952 Olympics, just eighteen years old, Milt competed in the grueling two-day, ten-event decathlon and won the silver medal. Four years later, at the Melbourne Olympics, Milt competed in the decathlon and took home the gold medal. Not limited to track-and-field events, he went on to play football for the NFL's Cleveland Browns. Milt, a member of the the National Track and Field Hall of Fame and the U.S. Olympic Hall of Fame, has spent over twenty years using his unique experiences in his work as a motivational speaker.

When things go wrong—as they will! And the times get tough—as they do! If you are going to win—as you wish! Keep your eye on the prize—as you must!

BOB MATHIAS

Bob Mathias was an accomplished high school athlete in basketball and football, but it was in track and field where he shone. After setting more than twenty high school records in the shot put, discus throw, high hurdles, and high jump, Bob's coach suggested that he try out for the 1948 London Olympic decathlon event. After a grueling competition that was performed in pelting rain and deep mud, Bob, at just seventeen, became the youngest man ever to win an Olympic gold medal. In the 1952 Games, held in Helsinki, Finland, Bob again set a record by becoming the first repeat decathlon winner. Despite a pulled thigh muscle, Bob won the decathlon by the largest margin in U.S. history. Throughout his athletic career Bob entered and won eleven decathlons, including the AAU national championships, 1948–50 and in 1952.

A winner never quits—a quitter never wins.

Milt Campbell Enterprise

WHEN THINGS GO WRONG — AS THEY WILL!
AND THE TIMES GET TOUGH — AS THEY DO!
IF YOU ARE GOING TO WIN — AS YOU WISH!
KEEP YOUR EYE ON THE PRIZE —
                                    AS YOU MUST!

Milt Campbell
"52" "56"

BOB MATHIAS

A winner — never quits —
A quitter never wins .

Bob Mathias
USA

As the 1976 Montreal Olympic Games approached, international gymnasts had heard that the fourteen-year-old Nadia Comaneci from Romania would be a formidable opponent, but no one suspected that the four-foot-ten athlete would make Olympic history. Nadia's flawless performance won her the first perfect score of ten in international gymnastic history. As the week went on the perfect scores kept coming. She amassed seven perfect tens on her way to winning three golds, one silver, and one bronze medal. Nadia also became the first Romanian to win an Olympic gymnastic gold medal. In 1980, Nadia arrived at the Moscow Olympic Games and once again dominated the competition, winning two gold medals for her performances in the beam and the floor events. Throughout Nadia's twelve-year career she was awarded thirty-one perfect scores of ten.

Don't pray for an easy life. Pray to be a strong person.

N A D I A   C O M A N E C I

„ Don't pray for a easy life
Pray to be a strong person "

Nadia Comaneci

Born in Chicago, Illinois, in 1958, Bart Conner is one of the most accomplished American gymnasts. A junior champion in 1972 and Pan American champion in 1975, Bart was the youngest member of the U.S. Olympic men's gymnastics team. Competing in the pommel horse event in 1979, Bart became the only American ever to win a gold medal at a World Cup event. Even though he was the top qualifier in the 1980 Olympic trials, Bart did not compete due to the U.S. boycott of the Moscow Olympics. He reappeared at the 1984 Games, winning the gold medal in the parallel bars with two perfect scores of ten.

In order to succeed in life you must find your F.O.C.U.S.

F **Find what your talents are**

O **Observe your mentors**

C **Challenge yourself (set goals)**

U **Utilize your resources**

S **Strive to make a difference**

BART CONNER EDUCATIONAL PROGRAMS, INC.

In order to succeed in life
you must find your
F.O.C.U.S.

F find what your talents are

O observe your mentors

C challenge yourself (set goals)

U utilize your resources

S strive to make a difference

Focus.

Bart Conner

Wayne Gretzky, an icon in professional hockey, is often referred to as "the Great One." His professionalism, his ability to keep his eye on the puck during the most confusing of on-ice melees, and his boy-next-door personality have all made Wayne a favorite with players and fans. Playing professionally since he was sixteen years old, Wayne has accrued sixty-one National Hockey League records, nine MVP trophies, nine Ross Memorial trophies for top scoring, and an Associated Press Award for Male Athlete of the Decade. He is the NHL's career scoring leader, played in eighteen consecutive all-star games, and was an all-star game MVP three times. In the late 1970s, Wayne played for the Edmonton Oilers of the World Hockey Association. The WHA folded and Wayne was a major part of the NHL's decision to allow the Oilers into the league. Today, Wayne is a member of the NHL's New York Rangers, a devoted husband, and father of three.

Failing to prepare is preparing to fail.

WAYNE D. GRETZKY

Failing To Prepare
is
Preparing To Fail

Wayne Gretzky
99

In a sport not always known for its finesse, hockey player Cam Neely combined tremendous power with an intricate and light scoring touch. Cam played professional hockey for thirteen years until he was forced to retire due to an injury. Playing for the Boston Bruins for ten years, Cam led the Bruins in scoring for several years and was only the second player in Bruins history to score back-to-back fifty-goal seasons. Today Cam spends much of his time with the Cam Neely Foundation, a charitable organization that promotes cancer awareness and research, and with the Neely House, a home away from home for cancer patients who are undergoing treatment at New England Medical Center, in Boston.

I have learned over the years that although there are many obstacles thrown in our path to reaching our goals, it is important that we try to overcome them. Determination and perseverance are the keys to success. Never lose sight of the simple yet important things in life; for it is those things that allow us to find inner peace and happiness.

"I have learned over the years that although there are many obstacles thrown in our path to reaching our goals, it is important that we try to overcome them. Determination and perseverance are the keys to success. Never lose sight of the simple, yet important things in life; for it is those things that allow us to find inner peace and happiness."

Olympic softball champion Dot Richardson uses her inspirational stories of athletic achievement in her work as a motivational speaker, author, and child advocate. Three-time Pan American gold medalist, four-time world champion, and winner of a 1996 Olympic gold medal for softball, Dot has received numerous awards and acknowledgments. In college at UCLA, Dot was three-time NCAA all-American and was named the NCAA's Player of the Decade for the 1980s. She was nominated for the Sullivan Award for Outstanding Amateur Athlete in the United States four times and named Female Athlete of the Year by the National Athlete Awards in 1997. Currently, she is nearing completion of her postdoctoral residency in orthopedic surgery, and is building the Softball Association, in Orlando, Florida, in order to teach and encourage young female softball players. She is also the sponsor of her own softball team for children ten and under.

The Most Important Thing I Know About The Spirit of Sport . . .
It instills in us the ability to recognize and appreciate the talents of others as well as the gifts that we have been given and the ability to work with others as a team. It also allows us to face the challenges of competition, learn from our successes and failures, altogether making us true champions in life.

Dot Richardson Softball Series, Inc.

"Fastpitch Softball - Play The Game Because You Love It!!"

The Most Important Thing I know About
The Spirit of Sport...

"It instills in us the ability to recognize and
appreciate the talents of others as well as the
gifts that we have been given and the ability
to work with others as a team. It also allows
us to face the challenges of competition, learn
from our successes and failures altogether
making us true champions in life."

Dr. Dot Richardson

Dot Richardson
#1
USA
Olympic
Gold '96

Paul Petzoldt, considered the Father of Outdoor Leadership and Wilderness Education in the United States, is renowned for his many mountaineering achievements and his contribution to wilderness conservation, education, and safety in the wild outdoors. As a mountaineer, Paul made his first ascent of Grand Teton at the age of sixteen. He went on to found the first school of mountaineering and to establish a climbing guide service in a national park. Paul has developed many climbing techniques still used today, such as the Climbing Signal System, sliding middle man snow technique, and high-attitude energy-conserving technique. A member of the first American Expedition to Kharakorum (K2) in 1938, he climbed to a record 26,000 feet without auxiliary oxygen. As an educator, Paul was the first chief instructor of Outward Bound in the United States. He founded the National Outdoor Leadership School and cofounded the Wilderness Education Association.

Paul's books include *The Wilderness Handbook*, *The New Wilderness Handbook*, and *Teton Tales*. At ninety, he frequently lectures at schools and universities across the United States, instructs his programs in Maine, and writes daily.

Know what you know and know what you don't know. Know if you don't turn back you will never reach 90.

Paul K. Petzoldt

Know what you Know
And Know what you
don't know.
Know if you don't
turn back you will
never reach 90.

Paul Petzoldt

World-class wrestler and coach John Smith has consistently brought recognition to a sport that is too often overlooked. In 1987, the Oklahoma native won his first of six world championships. He went on to win an Olympic gold medal and world freestyle championship in 1989–91 and in 1992 he won his second Olympic gold medal. Throughout his illustrious career, John has also won two Pan American gold medals, two Goodwill Games gold medals, and five U.S. titles. In 1992, John was named coach at Oklahoma State University, where he has led his team to numerous team and individual national titles. In 1997, he coached the U.S. World Cup team to a gold medal. For his numerous contributions to Olympic wrestling John was honored as one of the one hundred Olympians of all time at the 1996 Olympics.

Win or lose you will never regret working hard, making sacrifices, being disciplined or focusing too much. Success is measured by what we have done to prepare for competition.

DAN GABLE

Dan Gable, member of the Olympic Hall of Fame, is an example of the benefits of hard work and dedication. As a young man Dan set his sights on the 1972 Olympic Games. Practicing seven hours a day, seven days a week, he achieved numerous awards on the way to the Olympics. At Iowa State, in his weight division, Dan was the NCAA wrestling champion in 1968 and 1969, the AAU featherweight champion in 1969 and lightweight champion in 1970, and the world and Pan American champion in 1971. At the 1972 Olympics, Dan won a gold medal and became the only wrestler to win without surrendering a single point. After retiring from professional competition in 1972, Dan established a formidable reputation as the University of Iowa coach, where his teams have won fifteen NCAA championships.

Practice what you know today along with learning something new, then practice it all over again.

OKLAHOMA STATE WRESTLING
"A TRADITION OF EXCELLENCE"

Win or Lose you will Never REGRET
WORKING HARD, MAKING Sacrifices,
Being Discipline OR focusing to
MUCH. Success is MEASURED
By WHAT WE HAVE DONE TO
PREPARE FOR COMPETITION—

John W. Smith

IOWA WRESTLING

Iowa Wrestling
The University of Iowa
223 Carver-Hawkeye Arena
Iowa City, Iowa 52242-1020

(319) 335-9405

"Practice what you know today
along with learning something new
then practice it all over again"

Dan Gable

SARA DECOSTA

While Olympic gold medalist Sara DeCosta was growing up in a small town in Rhode Island, her older brother used to convince her to be goalie for his hockey games. That early practice sparked a love of hockey in Sara that has driven her to break gender barriers and to win international medals. In 1995, she played for the U.S. Women's National Junior Team and in 1996, Sara entered Providence College, where she earned an honorable mention in the Eastern College Athletic Conference. Two years later, at the Winter Olympics in Nagano, Sara was goalie for the Olympic gold medal women's hockey team. Currently, she is a college student and the lead campaign spokesperson for Rhode Island's Highway Safety Campaign, aimed at increasing motor vehicle seat belt use.

Reach for the stars . . . There are no limits!!!

MIKE ERUZIONE

Massachusetts native Mike Eruzione was the third leading hockey scorer in Boston University history, the best defensive forward in the East for four consecutive years, and part of a four-time Eastern Collegiate Championship hockey team. Mike has played on two U.S. national teams and for the International Hockey League, but he is most remembered for leading the 1980 U.S. Olympic hockey team to victory. During the last few moments of a remarkably close game, Mike, the team captain, scored the goal that resulted in a U.S. victory against the Soviet Union. The fans were ecstatic and Mike and his teammates were inducted into the U.S. Olympic Hall of Fame. Since winning the gold, Mike broadcasts both Winter and Summer Olympic Games and raises funds for the U.S. Olympic Committee. He is also the director of development for athletics and assistant hockey coach at Boston University.

The spirit of sport is about trying to be the best you can be, it's about setting goals and having fun striving to achieve them. It's also about understanding the value of work—without a strong work ethic you will not be successful.

SARA DeCOSTA
1998 WOMEN'S ICE HOCKEY
OLYMPIC GOLD

"REACH FOR THE STARS...
THERE ARE NO LIMITS!"

Boston University

THE SPIRIT OF SPORT IS ABOUT TRYING
TO BE THE BEST YOU CAN BE, IT'S ABOUT SETTING
GOALS AND HAVING FUN STRIVING TO ACHIEVE THEM.
IT'S ALSO ABOUT UNDERSTANDING THE VALUE OF WORK.
WITHOUT A STRONG WORK ETHIC YOU WILL NOT BE
SUCCESSFUL.

MATT BIONDI

At the 1984 Los Angeles Olympic Games, eighteen-year-old Matt won his first Olympic gold medal in the 400-meter relay. Then in 1988 Matt blazed into the Seoul Olympic Games, winning seven medals including a gold medal as the anchor in both the 400- and 800-meter freestyle relays and in the 400-meter medley relay, an individual gold medal in the 50-meter freestyle and the 100-meter freestyle, a silver medal in the 100-meter butterfly, and a bronze medal in the 200-meter freestyle. In the 1992 Olympics, Matt won two team gold medals, in the 4×100-meter freestyle and in the 4×100-meter medley relay, as well as a silver in the 50-meter freestyle.

Persistence can change failure into extraordinary achievement.

AMY VAN DYKEN

Four-time Olympic swimming gold medalist Amy Van Dyken was a frail and sickly child due to her severe asthma condition. She took up swimming to improve her lung capacity and pushed herself past the confines of her illness. At the 1996 Olympic Games, she won four gold medals in the 50-meter freestyle, the 100-meter butterfly, the 400-meter freestyle relay, and the 400-meter medley relay.

The most important lesson I've learned from sports is how to be not only a gracious winner, but a good loser as well. Not everyone wins all the time, as a matter of fact, *no one* wins all the time. Winning is the easy part, losing is really tough. But, you learn more from one loss than you do from a million wins. You learn a lot about sportsmanship. I mean, it's really tough to shake the hand of someone who just beat you, and it's even harder to do it with a smile. If you can learn to do this and push through that pain, you will remember what that moment is like the next time you win and have a better sense of how those competitors around you feel. This experience will teach you a lot on and off the field!

Persistence can change failure into extraordinary achievement!

Matt Biondi
Olympian
1984, 88, 92

Amy Van Dyken
Olympic Champion Swimmer

The most important lesson I've learned from sports is how to be not only a gracious winner, but a good looser as well. Not everyone wins all the time, as a matter of fact - no one wins all the time. Winning is the easy part, loosing is really tough. But, you learn more from one loss than you do from a million wins. You learn a lot about sportsmanship. I mean, its really tough to shake the hand of someone who just beat you, and its even harder to do it with a smile. If you can learn to do this - and push through that pain, you will remember what that moment is like the next time you win and have a better sense of how those competitors around you feel. This experience will teach you a lot on and off the fields!

Amy Van Dyken

The golf pro known as "Slammin' " Sammy Snead was born in the Virginia hills in 1912. Although his family did not have much money, Sam's imagination inspired him to build his own set of golf clubs out of horse buggy whips, discarded iron heads, and parts of an old swamp tree. Sam practiced endlessly, turned pro, and garnered a great deal of attention due to his huge and powerful drives. His amazing sixty-year professional career is a feat that is unmatched by anyone in professional golfing history. During his career Sam accumulated over 140 victories on American tours and almost 50 victories on international tours. The young boy whose first set of clubs were made from riding crops and an old tree grew up to win some of the most prestigious tournaments in professional golf, including three Masters, three PGA championships, and one British Open.

Never quit.

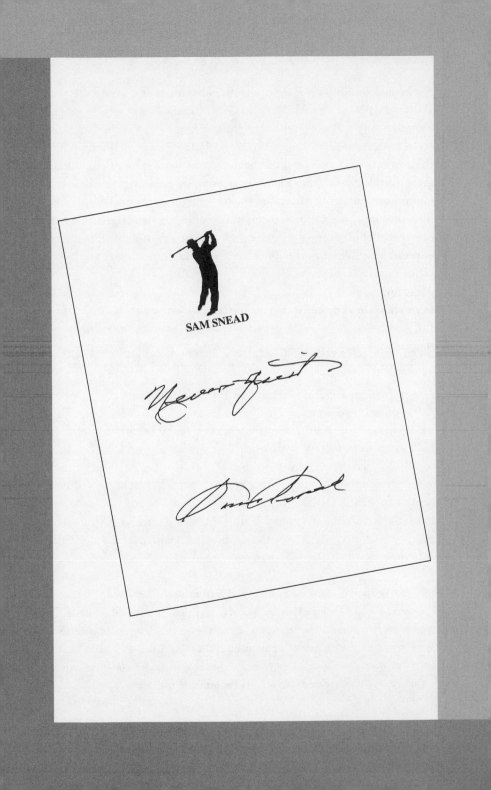

SAM SNEAD

JEAN-CLAUDE KILLY

Jean-Claude Killy grew up in the French Alps village of Val d'Isere. At the 1968 Grenoble Olympic Games, Jean-Claude won the dangerous downhill alpine event by eight hundredths of a second and his second event, the giant slalom, by a comfortable margin. Winning the third event, the slalom, would mean that he would become only the second triple alpine winner in twelve years. The race began with zero-visibility fog and contestants begging the judges to postpone the race. But the race went on as scheduled and Austrian Karl Schranz appeared to beat Jean-Claude. However, at the last minute, judges discovered that Schranz had missed a gate and Jean-Claude was proclaimed the winner.

Every day you must do better than the day before—fast.

ANDREA MEAD LAWRENCE

During the 1952 Oslo Olympics, American Andrea Lawrence stunned everyone by her extraordinary performance in the women's giant slalom. In an event usually won by tenths of a second, Andrea raced to victory with a full two-second lead on her competitors. In the slalom event, while she was in the lead of the first round, Andrea's ski caught a gate, forcing her to backtrack the course and finish the first round in fourth place. In the second round, she avoided mishaps and won the race by eight tenths of a second. Ultimately, Andrea beat the odds, won the gold medal, and became the first American to win two alpine skiing gold medals.

The spirit of sport is really the essence and ideal of all our human efforts. It is the exercising and joining of our individual energy with those of others in furthering the human race. Thus, competition strikes me as being *for* one another, and not against. I see it as participation, an unusual teamwork. Each contribution of spiritual and physical vitality establishes new plateaus from which others may thrust. It is a shared current; it is important to play well.

Every day, you must do
better than the day before.

... fast.

Killy

the SPIRIT of SPORT is really the
essence and ideal of all our
human efforts. It is the exercising
and joining of our individual energy
with those of others in furthering the
human race. Thus, COMPETITION STRIKES me
as being FOR one another, and not
against. I see it as participation, an
unusual TEAMWORK. Each contribution of
spiritual and physical vitality establishes
new plateaus from which others may
thrust. It is a shared current; IT IS
IMPORTANT to PLAY WELL.

MARK SPITZ

Swimming legend and future Olympic gold medalist, Mark Spitz already had accumulated seventeen national age group swimming records. Mark entered the 1968 Olympics in Mexico City as one of America's most outstanding amateur athletes. He surpassed the public's expectations by winning two gold, one silver, and one bronze medal. At the University of Indiana, in addition to completing his studies, he won four national and two college championships, and set seven world records and two U.S. records. In 1971, he was honored with the prestigious Sullivan Award for outstanding amateur athlete. At the 1972 Olympics in Munich, as fans around the world watched, Mark won seven swimming gold medals, establishing seven new world records. He remains tied for the most gold medals (nine) won by an American athlete. Mark is one of the most sought-after motivational speakers, appearing in numerous television commercials for several major companies. Recently, collaborating with the Merrill Lynch Financial Group, Mark has helped raise more than $1 million for the U.S. Olympic Committee.

I'm trying to do the best I can. I'm not concerned about tomorrow, but with what goes on today.

SUSIE O'NEILL

Susie O'Neill has become Australia's golden girl. Holding over thirty Australian swimming titles, in January 1998 she became the world, Olympic, and Commonwealth champion in the 200-meter butterfly. The first Australian swimmer to win a gold medal in the 200-meter butterfly event, Susie has never competed on an international level without bringing home a medal. Ranking as one of Australia's premier Olympic performers, Susie won three medals at the 1996 Atlanta Olympic Games: a gold in the 200-meter butterfly, a silver in the 4×100 medley relay, and a bronze in the 4×200-meter race. Susie was named the 1996 Female Australian Olympian of the Year and Australia's Swimmer of the Year in 1996 and in 1997.

If you're not happy, you can't perform at your best!!

I'M TRYING TO DO THE BEST I CAN.
I'M NOT CONCERNED ABOUT TOMORROW, BUT
WITH WHAT GOES ON TODAY.
— Cal Smith

The most important thing I know:
If you're not happy,
You can't perform at your best!!

Susie O'Neill

Benita Fitzgerald Mosley, eight-time national champion and fifteen-time all-American, is the second American and the only African-American woman to win an Olympic gold medal in the 100-meter hurdles. After winning a Pan American gold medal in 1983 and an Olympic gold medal in 1984, and several other major championships, Benita retired from competition. In 1991, she became regional director for the Special Olympics International in Washington, D.C. There she helped raise public awareness and appreciation for the Special Olympics. Two years later, Benita directed the marketing division of the Atlanta Committee for the Olympic Games. Currently Benita is the director of all U.S. Olympic training centers for the U.S. Olympic Committee, and president of the Women's Sports Foundation. This nonprofit organization promotes opportunities for girls and women in sports and fitness.

The Bible says to "run in such a way as to win the prize." Excellence is giving a gold medal effort in all that you endeavor . . . at school, work, home and on the playing field.

Benita Fitzgerald Mosley
Director, U.S. Olympic Training Centers

The Bible says to "run in such a way as to win the prize".

Excellence is giving a GOLD MEDAL effort in all that you endeavor... at school, work, home and on the playing field.

Benita Fitzgerald Mosley

1984 Olympic Gold Medalist, 100 meter hurdles

GENE STALLINGS

Gene Stallings's winning record as a football coach evokes images of someone who is relentless and demanding. While that may be true, through his son, Johnny, Gene has learned to add more warmth and caring to his life. In 1962, the coach learned that his newborn son had Down's syndrome. Gene was plagued with decisions about how to best care for Johnny. While most people urged him to institutionalize his son, Gene would not consider it. After stints in the NFL coaching for the Cardinals and Cowboys, Gene returned with his family to Tuscaloosa, Alabama. There he concentrated on caring for his son while at the same time coaching the University of Alabama Crimson Tide to five bowl appearances. He also produced Alabama's first undefeated season in 1992. Johnny, a familiar face at the Alabama games, is always warmly greeted by both players and fans.

You can't go wrong by doing right.

BART STARR

Bart Starr first came to the attention of the football world as the University of Alabama's quarterback. Drafted by the Green Bay Packers in 1956, Bart shared time with other quarterbacks for three years before taking over the position. Over the next eight years, Bart led the Packers to two Super Bowl victories, five league titles, and six division championships. Bart was named the NFL's Most Valuable Player in 1966, the MVP of Super Bowl I and II, and he was inducted into both the Green Bay Packers Hall of Fame and the Pro Football Hall of Fame. Currently he is chairman of Healthcare Realty Services, a fully integrated health care real estate company.

Athletic competition clearly defines the unique power of our attitude.

You can't go wrong
by doing right.

Gene Stallings

Athletic competition clearly
defines the unique power
of our Attitude.

Bart Starr

BOB HAYES

Winning the title World's Fastest Human, traditionally bestowed upon the fastest sprinter, is even more impressive when looked at in conjunction with Bob Hayes's usual slow starts. In a race where the start is usually vital, sprinter Bob Hayes, a relatively poor starter, was the first to run better than 6 seconds in the 60-yard dash and the first to run 9.1 seconds in the 100-yard dash. After tying a world record in the 220-yard dash, Bob victoriously competed in the 1964 Olympics, where he won the 100-meter gold medal. As part of the Olympic 400-meter relay team, he won another gold medal and set another world record. After the Olympics, Bob played twelve seasons as a wide receiver with the Dallas Cowboys. He was later inducted into the National Track and Field Hall of Fame.

Somewhere on this earth we all stand a chance, it's just knowing where we must stand. As a runner you must stay one step ahead of the pack. It's blood, sweat, sometimes tears.

AL OERTER

Al Oerter arrived at the 1956 Melbourne Olympics unnoticed, overwhelmed, and scared, but he won gold and set an Olympic record. Four years later, on his fifth and final throw, Al won gold again. When the 1964 Tokyo Games rolled around, Al had doubts about his upcoming performance. A cervical disk injury and torn rib cage cartilage doubled him over in pain. Al threw the discus two hundred feet and one inch, achieving another gold medal and Olympic record. Unbelievably, Al went on to the 1968 Mexico City Games to win another gold medal and set another Olympic record. This shy and modest man is the first athlete ever to win four gold medals in the same event.

Those that succeed push just a little harder—each day—and those that don't wish they had years later.

Somewhere on this Earth
We all stand a chance;
It's just knowing where
We must stand.
As A Runner you Must
stay one step ahead of
the pack,
It's Blood, Sweat Sometime
Tears

Bob Hayes

THOSE THAT SUCCEED PUSH
JUST A LITTLE HARDER - EACH DAY -
AND THOSE THAT DON'T WISH THEY
HAD YEARS LATER.

Al Oerter
Olympic Gold 1956-60-64-68

A graduate of Florida State University's School of Law in 1978, Tony La Russa passed the bar exam in December 1979, making him one of five lawyer/managers in baseball history. He is regarded by his peers as one of baseball's top managers and has been honored with three Manager of the Year Awards, five American League Western Division titles, three American League championships, and one World Series championship. After playing in the major leagues and managing in the minor leagues, Tony took over the Chicago White Sox in 1979. In 1983, he was named Manager of the Year and the White Sox won the Western Division championship. In 1986, Tony joined the Oakland Athletics and with the A's Tony became a managing legend. In seventh place when he came aboard, he quickly brought them to third place. After their second third-place win, Tony and the Oakland Athletics won three consecutive pennants and the 1989 World Series. Tony was voted Manager of the Year in 1983, 1988, 1992, and 1996, the year he joined the St. Louis Cardinals.

A healthy attitude getting ready for a competition, participating in the competition and reviewing it afterwards is to have "NO REGRETS." Translates into doing all that you can to get ready and dedicate all the physical and mental effort that you have to the game!

FROM THE DESK OF . . .

TONY LA RUSSA

A HEALTHY ATTITUDE GETTING READY FOR A COMPETITION, PARTICIPATING IN THE COMPETITION AND REVIEWING IT AFTERWARDS IS TO HAVE

"NO REGRETS"

TRANSLATES INTO DOING ALL THAT YOU CAN TO GET READY AND DEDICATE ALL THE PHYSICAL AND MENTAL EFFORT THAT YOU HAVE TO THE GAME!

Tony La Russa

AL UNSER, JR.

Two-time Indianapolis 500 winner, Al Unser, Jr., never questioned that he would race cars; he just did not know that he would spend much of his professional career racing against his dad. In 1981, he came to national attention by winning the SuperVee championship, setting six track records, and becoming Sports Car Club of America's Rookie of the Year. Al won his first Indy 500 race in 1984. For the next several years, Al was neck and neck for the national championships with his father, race car professional Al Unser, Sr. At the International Race of Champions in 1986, Al narrowly beat his father and won the world-class event. Al Jr. went on to win the 1990 national driving championship and the 1992 Indy 500.

The most important thing I know is to always try your best and put love and faith in God and his son Jesus Christ. Effort=Results.

PATTY MOISE

Florida native Patty Moise has been drawn to the excitement of fast cars since she was a child. Growing up, she loved watching her father, stock car racer Milton Moise, race. By the time she turned sixteen, Patty had her sights set on fast cars and challenging courses. Although stock car racing is traditionally a male-dominated sport, Patty has turned her gender into an advantage rather than an impediment. In 1996, she and her husband founded and ran their own Busch Grand National Team. Over the course of her career, Patty has accumulated 130-plus NASCAR Busch series starts and has broken the women's one-lap closed-course speed record at 217.498 mph. Currently she is driving for Winston Cup car owner Michael Waltrip and is being sponsored by Rhodes Furniture, a Virginia-based company.

In sports and in business it's good to be goal oriented and relentless in your pursuit of your goals. However, in life it's not all about the destination—it's really about the journey. So it's important to enjoy the journey, and in the end, to be able to be proud of the person you've become along the way.

from the desk of **AL UNSER JR.**

The Most Important thing
I know is to always try
your best and Put love
and Faith in God and his
son Jesus Christ. Effort = Results

Al Unser Jr.

MOISE-SAWYER MSM MOTORSPORTS

In sports and in business it's good to
be goal oriented and relentless in your
pursuit of your goals. However, in life
it's not all about the destination — it's
really about the journey. So it's
important to enjoy the journey, and
in the end, to be able to be proud
of the person you've become along the
way.

Gary Moise

DICK BUTTON

ooking at the overweight eleven-year-old, Dick Button's first figure skating coach told him he would never be any good. No one imagined that the young boy who had just received his first pair of figure skates would go on to set world records in competitive figure skating. By the age of twenty-three, Dick, who had long since shed his baby fat and his shortsighted first coach, had won seven national championships and five world championships. In 1948, as a Harvard freshman, he competed in his first Olympic Games, performing a flawless double axel and winning a gold medal. At the 1952 Olympic Games he won his second gold medal, then used his skating skills and knowledge to become an expert commentator for televised skating events. In 1981 he was awarded the first Emmy Award given for an Outstanding Sports Personality. He created The World Professional Figure Skating Championship competitions, giving opportunities to all skaters. His World Professional Championship is the most popular figure-skating event of the competitive season.

Education, no matter how esoteric, will someday, somewhere, someplace be of great use.

TARA LIPINSKI

ara Lipinski is a bright young woman whose hobbies include sewing, visiting children's hospitals, and winning world championship figure-skating titles. In 1996, at just age fifteen, Tara became the youngest woman to win an Olympic skating title. She had made many sacrifices to win her Olympic gold medal. In addition to the endless hours of practice, Tara had to move away from her family and friends so she could obtain the elite coaching necessary to train to her potential. However, her sacrifices have paid off. Besides Tara's winning the world championship title at fourteen, her extremely difficult jumps have pushed figure-skating standards to a new level.

Always believe in yourself!

RICHARD T. BUTTON

Education, no matter how esoteric, will someday, somewhere, someplace be of great use.

Dick Button

Tara K. Lipinski

Always believe
in yourself!

Tara Lipinski

Grete Waitz of Norway had already won four world cross-country titles in the 3,000-meter event, when in 1978 she decided to try a marathon. Without any marathon training Grete not only won the New York City Marathon, she set a new women's world record. Encouraged and surprised by her success, Grete trained and won eight more NYC Marathons. She set four world records in the marathon event and won a silver medal in the 1984 Olympic Games. Grete does not compete anymore, but she remains involved in the marathon event, helping and inspiring others to cross the finish line.

Without goals life becomes meaningless, boring and dull. Having goals is important, but they are useful only if you believe in them wholeheartedly and identify yourself with them. You should set your goals yourself and for yourself.

Grete Waitz
Birgitte Hammers vei 15 G.
1169 Oslo 11, Norway

Without goals life becomes meaningless,
boring and dull. Having goals is important,
but they are useful only if you believe
in them wholeheartedly and identify yourself
with them.
You should set your goals yourself
and for yourself.

Grete Waitz

Zoe Koplowitz, a native New Yorker and the last competitor to cross the finish line in the 1998 Boston Marathon, is an inspiration to us all. Suffering from multiple sclerosis, Zoe finished the marathon in 30 hours and 53 minutes on her special shock-absorbing crutches. Zoe, who spends most of her time as a motivational spokesperson, is the first woman with multiple sclerosis to start and complete ten consecutive marathons. Her 30:53 Boston Marathon set the world record for the slowest marathon in the history of women's running. Ms. Koplowitz is an award-winning author of *The Winning Spirit—Life Lessons Learned in Last Place*.

Winning is not always or necessarily about being first. It *can* be, but it doesn't have to be. I believe that winning is about doing whatever it is that calls to your soul—from the bottom of your heart with everything you've got! Win, lose, or draw . . . first place or last . . . in my book this is what makes a winner. Blessings . . .

BILL RODGERS

Bill Rodgers did some running while in college at Wesleyan University, but nothing that would indicate he was on the brink of being a marathon record breaker. When his Triumph motorcycle was stolen, he began running to work. Soon he was running over one hundred miles a week. In 1975, Bill ran in the International Cross-Country Championship, placing third, the best ever for an American runner. He won the New York City Marathon four consecutive times between 1976 and 1980 and the Boston Marathon four times in 1975 and 1978 through 1980. Bill competed in the 1976 Olympic Games but was unable to compete in 1980 due to the U.S. boycott of the Moscow Games. Bill is currently one of the top runners in the world today in the fifty-plus age group.

When I think of excellence I think of it as individuals putting forth their best effort in their daily lives and in one way or another trying to use that effort as a message of goodwill to share.

The Winning Spirit
Life Lessons
Learned
In
Last Place

WINNING is NOT always or NECESSARILY about being first. It can be, but it doesn't have TO BE.

I believe THAT WINNING is about doing whatever it is THAT calls To your soul — from The bottom of your heart WiTH Everything you've GOT !!

WIN, lose or draw .. FIRST place or last .. IN my BOOK This is what makes a WINNER.

Blessings ...   ZOE

When I think of excellence I think of it as an individual putting forth their best effort in their daily lives and in one way or another trying to use that effort in a message of goodwill to share.

Bill Rodgers

Aviator Jeana Yeager is one of the most accomplished aviators in U.S. history. She made history as part of the two-person crew that flew the *Voyager* in a globe-circling, nonstop, no-refuel flight. This flight was hugely significant because it was the last remaining milestone in aviation. Never before had anyone flown the circumference distance of the Earth nonstop. In 1987, this Texas native became the first woman in history to be awarded the Collier Trophy, the most coveted award in aviation. Jeana has also received the Presidential Citizen's Medal of Honor from President Reagan and the Royal Aero Club's gold medal, presented by Prince Andrew, Duke of York, and by Sarah Ferguson, Duchess of York.

Anything is possible; even the impossible.

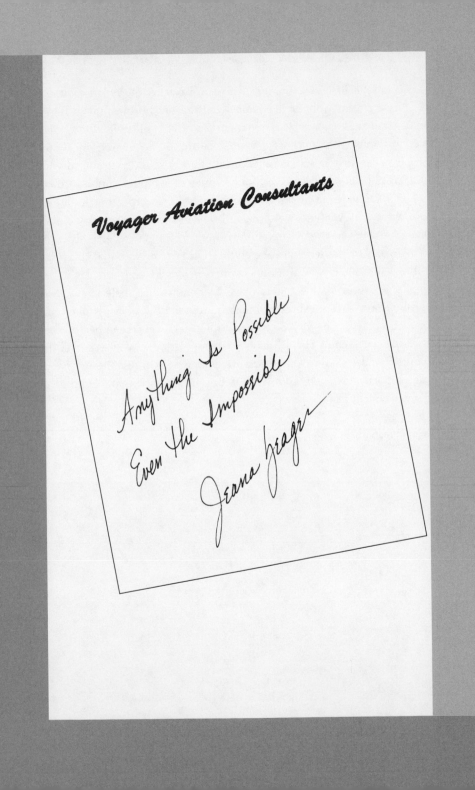

Voyager Aviation Consultants

Anything Is Possible
Even the Impossible

Jeana Yeager

Billie Jean King, the holder of a record twenty Wimbledon titles, has proven both her tennis prowess and her business savvy. Born in Long Beach, California, November 22, 1943, Billie Jean won her first Wimbledon title at age seventeen in a doubles match. In 1966, she won her first of six Wimbledon singles titles. She went on to win ten Wimbledon doubles titles, four Wimbledon mixed doubles titles, the U.S. Open four times, the Australian Open, and the French Open. But these achievements were marked by a gender disparity that Billie Jean could not ignore. Bothered that the prize money received by pro female players was less than one eighth of that offered to male players, Billie Jean helped found an all-women professional tour. Later, she challenged professional tennis player and notorious male chauvinist Bobby Riggs, and beat him in a match attended by more people than any other in the history of tennis. Billie Jean King, member of the International Tennis Hall of Fame and the National Women's Hall of Fame, founder of the Women's Sports Foundation and *Women's Sports* magazine, has changed professional tennis into a sport that exemplifies gender equality and appreciation.

Accept responsibility.

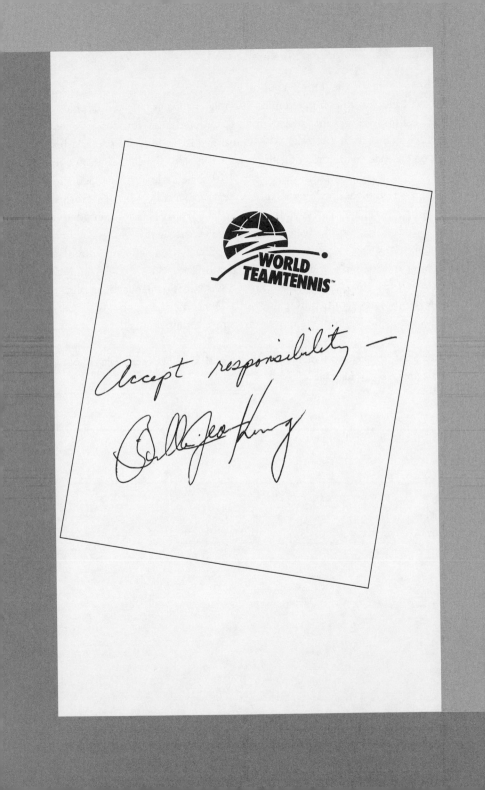

Accept responsibility —

Billie Jean King

Member of the Tennis Hall of Fame and the U.S. Army, Corporal Stan Smith competed in the prestigious Davis Cup tennis championships a remarkable twenty-four times, winning twenty-two times. He was nicknamed "Godzilla" because of his six-four stature and his immense strength, and what Stan lacked in finesse he made up for in aggression and discipline. In 1971 and 1972 he added a U.S. Open and then a Wimbledon title to his already expansive collection of victories. During his career he won thirty-nine singles titles, represented the United States for the Davis Cup for ten years, winning the coveted championship seven times. In addition, Smith won sixty-one doubles titles, and, now playing on the ATP Senior Tour, Stan is still winning. He is the U.S. Tennis Association's advisor/national coach of player development, a contributing editor to *Tennis* magazine, and, with Adidas shoes, designed the famous Stan Smith tennis shoe.

The most fulfilling and enduring aspect of a goal is not finally achieving it, but the *process* of getting there.

Stan Smith

The most fulfilling and enduring aspect of a goal is not finally achieving it, but the process of getting there.

Stan Smith

Six-time Olympic medalist Leon Stukelj, at one hundred years old, is the world's oldest living Olympic gold medalist. Leon was in attendance at the 1936 Berlin Olympic Games when Hitler paraded Nazi propaganda in front of the world. From Slovenia, Leon began competing before WWI when Slovenia was still part of the former Yugoslavia. In the 1920s, Leon invented the inverted iron cross, a move on the rings that is used in Olympic competition today. More than seventy years later, he still wakes up at 7 A.M. to walk and exercise. The Slovenian native credits his longevity to a combination of the physical and psychological discipline he learned from gymnastics training, along with the mental rigors of his law career. He was a practicing lawyer when he won two gold medals at the 1924 Paris Olympic Games. Leon won his third gold medal in the ring event at the 1928 Amsterdam Olympics. He was honored at the 1996 Olympic Games as one of the most influential Olympians in history, and his picture graces a stamp and a coin in his native Slovenia. On November 12, 1998, at his one-hundreth birthday celebration, Leon was personally invited to attend the 2000 Olympics in Sydney, Australia, by International Olympic Committee president Juan Antonio Samaranch. "I do not know in what condition I'd be in 2000," Mr. Stukelj said. "When 2000 comes, we'll talk again."

By cultivating the harmony of body and spirit all stages of life can be happy and fulfilling.

OLIMPIJSKI ZMAGOVALEC
CHAMPION OLYMPIQUE

Vsa obdobja življenja so lahko srečna le ob sočasnem kultiviranju ter harmoniji telesa in duha.

Leon Štukelj

By the age of twenty-one Shannon Miller has become the most decorated American gymnast, male or female, in history, having won more Olympic and world championship medals than any other American gymnast. She began gymnastics at the age of five in her hometown of Edmond, Oklahoma. At fourteen the years of practice and discipline paid off; she won two silver medals at the World Gymnastics Championships. The following year Shannon earned two silver medals and three bronze medals at the 1992 Olympic Games in Barcelona. Her Olympic success continued in 1996 as a member of "The Magnificent Seven," with whom she won two gold medals: team gold and for the first time for any American gymnast, gold in the balance beam.

Doing your best is more important than being the best.

An American gymnast had never won an Olympic gold medal on foreign soil, or had been awarded gold at a nonboycotted Games since the USSR joined the Olympic Movement in 1952. No one expected gymnast Trent Dimas to make the 1992 Olympic team. He had never won any significant international competition.

Just before midnight on August 2, in the last event in the men's gymnastics competition, the high bar finals, Trent Dimas completed every release smoothly and moved from one skill to another seemingly without effort. His landing was perfect. Although a medal placement hadn't been determined, he knew it was the best he could deliver. With a score of 9.875, Trent Dimas made gymnastics history. Dimas's achievement on the high bar secured the only gold medal at the XXV Olympiad for an American gymnast.

The embodiment of success is best stated in the Bible: "I have fought the good fight, I have finished the race, I have kept the faith." II Timothy 4:7

Shannon Miller

Doing your best is more
important than being the best.

Shannon Miller
'92 '96

The embodiment of success
is best stated in the Bible:
"I have fought the good fight,
I have finished the race, I
have kept the faith." II Timothy 4:7

Kerri Strug
Olympic Champion
Gymnastics XXVI Games

Winner of five Olympic medals, named Female Athlete of the Year by the Associated Press and Amateur Sportswoman of the Year by the Women's Sports Foundation, Jackie Joyner-Kersee is considered to be one of the world's greatest female athletes. While attending UCLA on an athletic scholarship, Jackie set college records of 22 feet 11.5 inches in the long jump and 6,718 points in the pentathon, and won the Broderick Cup, honoring her as the nation's most outstanding female college athlete. Battling asthma and chronic hamstring problems, Jackie won the heptathlon, a two-day, seven-event contest, nine times nationally and internationally by 1988. (The heptathlon champion is regarded as the finest all-around female athlete in the world.) At the 1988 Seoul Olympic Games, Jackie won that title and beat her own world record. Four days later she beat the Olympic record in the long jump and came home with two gold medals. In 1992, in Barcelona, she again beat her record, winning a gold medal in the heptathlon and a bronze medal in the long jump. Despite her health problems Jackie has persevered, becoming the first athlete, male or female, to win multievent medals in three Olympics.

Excellence is achieving the highest honor and remembering the dedication and hard work it took to achieve such an honor!!

Jackie Joyner-Kersee

Excellence is Achieving the
Highest honor And remembering
the dedication and the hardwork
it took to Achieve such
AN honor!!

Jacqueline J. Kersee

Sports manager, author, mother of two professional hockey players and the wife of another, Colleen Howe has written *My Three Hockey Players* and co-authored *And . . . Howe!*, an internationally bestselling autobiography of Colleen and her husband, Gordie. Colleen became the first female professional manager in sports, and also founded the Detroit Junior Red Wings, the first junior hockey program in the United States. Currently, Colleen spends much of her time leading her company, Power Play International Inc., in Traverse City, Michigan, and the Howe Foundation, a nonprofit organization she created whose mission is to improve the quality of life for children of all ages.

The Turtle Theory! Be hard on the outside and soft on the inside and willing to stick out your neck to get ahead!

Gordie Howe, considered by many to be the greatest all-around hockey player ever, began his professional hockey career in 1946, at age eighteen, never dreaming that in 1980 he would be the first grandfather playing professional hockey. Gordie has played an unprecedented six decades, and he ranks first for most goals, regular season games played (2,186), and most all-star appearances. In his thirty-two-season career with the Detroit Red Wings, Gordie was showered with honors. He led the Red Wings to four Stanley Cup championships and was named the NHL's Most Valuable Player six times. In 1974, Gordie became the first player to play any professional sport with his sons, Mark and Marty.

I always tell kids, you have two eyes and one mouth. Keep two open and one closed. You never learn anything if you're the one talking.

POWER PLAY INTERNATIONAL INC.

The Turtle Theory!

Be hard on the outside and soft on the inside and willing to stick out your neck to get ahead!

Colleen J. Lowe
Mrs. Hockey®

I always tell kids, you have two eyes and one mouth. — Keep two open and one closed.

You never learn anything if you're the one talking.

Gordie Howe
Mr. Hockey.

Greg Foster, champion runner and hurdler, competed internationally for sixteen years, holding a world record for fifteen of those years. While attending UCLA, Greg was the NCAA champion in the 200-meter event in 1979 and in the 110-meter hurdles in 1978 and 1980. After graduating, Greg focused on the hurdles and won three world championships and four national outdoor championships. Shortly after he won his first world championship, five of Greg's family members were killed in a tragic car accident. Struggling to recover from the enormous emotional blow, Greg continued to train. He became the first athlete to win three consecutive world championships in the 110-meter hurdles. In the 1984 Olympic Games Greg won a silver medal.

For the first quarter of our lives we watch, we learn and we follow the paths of those we love, honor, obey and respect. At one point in our lives we must take what we've seen, learned and patterned ourselves after, and transform that into a positive image of leadership for others to watch, learn and follow, until it is their turn to be the leader. "One is not a leader just because he is in the front." He must learn to lead!

G.B.M. Enterprises Inc.

For the first quarter of our lives we watch, we learn & we follow the paths of those we love honor, obey & respect. At one point in our lives we must take what weve seen, learned & patterned ourselves after, and transform that into a positive image of leadership for others to watch, learn & follow, until it is their turn to be the leader. "One is not a leader just because he is in the front" He must first learn to lead!

Gregory Easter
4x World Champion
Olympic Silver Medalist

Before Pat Williams assumed the reins of the Orlando Magic, for twelve years he was the general manager of the Philadelphia 76ers, including the 1983 season when they won the NBA championship. Before that, he was general manager for the Atlanta Hawks and Chicago Bulls. In 1996 Pat was named as one of the fifty most influential people in NBA history. President, co-founder, and general manager of the Orlando Magic, Pat Williams is credited with using his eye for talent and his remarkable marketing ability to motivate the Magic and bring them success and fame. Pat's unconventional style and outlandish antics have inspired the Orlando Magic, attracted premier players such as Shaquille O'Neal and Penny Hardaway, and helped lead them to the 1995 NBA finals. Nineteen of his teams went to the NBA playoffs and five have gone all the way to the finals. He has used his imaginative style and unique wit in writing seventeen popular motivational books, and he serves as one of America's top inspirational public speakers. Pat and his wife, Ruth, are the parents of nineteen children, including fourteen adopted children from South Korea, the Philippines, Romania, and Brazil.

Thoughts on Excellence I Learned from Walt Disney's Life & Career:

1. Think tomorrow (make today an investment in tomorrow).
2. Free up your imagination (we can usually do more than we ever thought we could).
3. Strive for lasting quality (don't cut corners; do everything the best you can the first time).
4. Stick-to-it-ivity-(don't quit too soon; hang in there).
5. Have fun!

★★★★★★★
Just wanted to bounce something off you!

Pat Williams — THOUGHTS OF EXCELLENCE / LEARNED FROM WALT DISNEY'S LIFE + CAREER.

1. THINK TOMORROW (MAKE TODAY AN INVESTMENT IN TOMORROW.)

2. FREE UP YOUR IMAGINATION (WE CAN USUALLY DO MORE THAN WE EVER THOUGHT WE COULD.)

3. STRIVE FOR LASTING QUALITY (DON'T CUT CORNERS; DO EVERYTHING THE BEST YOU CAN THE FIRST TIME.)

4. STICK-TO-IT-IVITY- (DON'T QUIT TOO SOON; HANG IN THERE.)

5. HAVE FUN!

Pat Williams
ORLANDO MAGIC

Orlando
MAGIC™

ALBERTO SALAZAR

As a child, world-class marathon runner Alberto Salazar emigrated from Cuba with his family to escape the Castro regime. In 1980 Alberto won his first of three New York Marathons, setting a marathon record in New York of 2:08:13. He then set his sights on the Boston Marathon, a race he had had the opportunity to watch as a teenager growing up in Massachusetts. In 1982, Alberto won the Boston Marathon in 2:08:52.

The most important thing about sports to me is how it helps us to be a better and stronger person, and live a more meaningful life. Learning to deal with adversity and setbacks in sports prepares us to deal with the certain curveballs that life will throw at us. If sports doesn't help us in this manner, it really doesn't have much long-term value.

JEAN DRISCOLL

Jean Driscoll's optimism and perseverance despite her use of a wheelchair has made her a world-renowned champion. In 1992, Jean set an American record and won a silver medal in the 800-meter exhibition event at the Olympic Games in Barcelona. Two years later at the world track-and-field championships, she won medals in the 10,000-meter, 5,000-meter, and 1,500-meter events. Jean won another silver medal at the 1996 Olympic Games in Atlanta. She added to her success at the Paralympic Games two weeks later by winning gold medals in the marathon and the 10,000-meter events, a silver in the 5,000-meter event, and a bronze in the 1,500-meter event. In addition to Jean's Olympic and Paralympic championships, she also has won seven Boston Marathons. Currently, she is a professional athlete, speaker and a volunteer assistant coach for the University of Illinois's wheelchair racing team.

Dream *big* and *work hard*! Your biggest limitations are the ones you place on yourself or allow others to place on you. Sure, very few people make it into the Olympics, the NBA/WNBA or other elite levels of life, *but* remember, there *are* people who make it!

The most important thing about sports to me is how it helps us to be a better and stronger person, and live a more meaningful life. Learning to deal with adversity and setbacks in sports prepares us to deal with the certain curveballs that life will throw at us. If sports doesn't help us in this manner, it really doesn't have much long term value.

— Alberto Salazar

USA

Dream <u>BIG</u> and Work Hard! Your biggest limitations are the ones you place on yourself or allow others to place on you. Sure, very few people make it into the Olympics, the NBA/WNBA or other elite levels of life, BUT remember, there <u>are</u> people who make it!

Jean Driscoll

KENDALL CROSS

During high school in Oklahoma, Kendall was state wrestling champion and was ranked fourth in the 1985 Junior Nationals. At Oklahoma State University, Kendall continued to improve, winning two NCAA championship medals. Throughout his professional career, Kendall has won numerous medals, including two World Cup medals, one U.S. Open International medal, and an Olympic gold medal. He was named the 1992 Outstanding Freestyle Wrestler and the 1996 USA Wrestling Freestyle champion. Currently he is an assistant wrestling coach at Harvard University and a volunteer for youth wrestling programs.

Intense desire sometimes creates not only its own opportunities, but its own talents as well!

JIMMY PEDRO

Fourth-degree black belt judo champion and 1996 Olympic bronze medalist Jimmy Pedro has his sights set on the 2000 Olympics in Sydney, Australia, where he hopes to add another medal to his array of awards. Coached by his father, Jimmy began judo at just six years of age and was a U.S. junior national champion ten times. At Brown University, he was twice a member of the all-ivy team and was two-time wrestling team captain. While at Brown he was twice named the USOC Male Athlete of the Year for judo, participated in the 1992 Olympics, and was winner of the 1990 and 1992 U.S. Open. Jimmy has been blazing a new path for U.S. judo athletes by becoming the first American to win the Paris Open, the Shoriki Cup, the Austria Open, and the World Masters in Germany.

There is no secret formula for success. All that is required is a lofty dream, hard work, the ability to see yourself achieving your dream, and a relentless desire to make it come true.

KENDALL CROSS
Olympic Gold Medalist
USA Wrestling

"Intense desire sometimes creates not only its own opportunities, but its own talents as well!"

Anonymous

Kendall Cross
Olympic Gold Medalist

There is no secret formula for success. All that is required is a lofty dream, hard work, the ability to see yourself achieving your dream, and a relentless desire to make it come true.

Jimmy Pedro

Rhode Island native, Special Olympics athlete, and advocate for the disabled, Henry Moretti has been involved in the Special Olympics for twenty-five years. As a child, Henry was enrolled in the Trudeau Center for the Retarded for recreational and social services. Through the center, he became involved with the Special Olympics and competed in his first meet at just twelve years old. Since then, Henry has competed, both nationally and internationally, in numerous sports including cross-country skiing, track and field, weight lifting, softball, baseball, soccer, and golf. At thirty-eight, Henry was the first Special Olympics athlete to serve as a member of the board of directors for the Rhode Island Special Olympics. In 1989 he began speaking out for Special Olympics as an Athlete for Outreach. In the broader community, Henry attends Partners in Policy Making, a Rhode Island state–funded advocacy organization for the disabled.

What I like about the spirit of sports is to compete and win medals and to be the best I can be.

Special Olympics
Rhode Island

What I like about the Spirit of Sports is to compete and win medals and to be the best I can be

Henry Moretti II

In college at the University of Seattle, Elgin Baylor, future member of the Basketball Hall of Fame, was an all-American forward, and ranked second scorer in the nation and third in the nation in rebounding. In 1958, Elgin joined the Los Angeles Lakers, bringing to the team not only his incredible scoring power but also his finesse in passing and rebounding. From 1960 to 1963, Elgin averaged more than 30 points a game. In 1965, he broke a kneecap; although he recovered from this injury, it affected his game. Still, through 1970, Elgin continued to score more than 20 points a game. In 1971, he retired, leaving behind an impressive record which includes a total of 23,149 points scored, 11,463 rebounds, and 3,650 assists. *USA Today* in January 1999 ranked Elgin one of ten greatest basketball palyers of all times.

Every time you compete, try harder to improve on your last performance. Give nothing short of your very best effort.

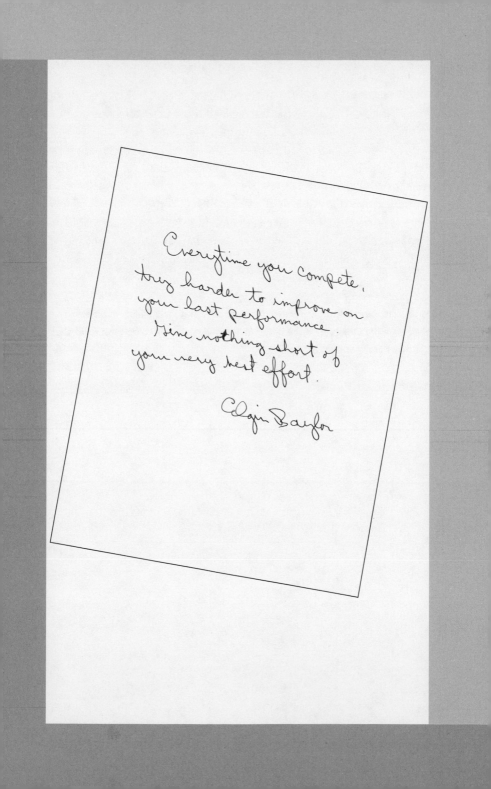

Everytime you compete,
try harder to improve on
your last performance.
Give nothing short of
your very best effort.

Elgin Baylor

Alternately known as the "Houdini of the Hardwood" and the "Mobile Magician," Basketball Hall of Famer Bob Cousy's spur-of-the-moment maneuvers and immense talent would leave opponents wondering what had happened to the ball. An all-American at Holy Cross, Bob joined the Boston Celtics in 1950. As a Celtic, Bob led the NBA in assists for eight years and helped lead his team to six championships. He was voted MVP in 1957, retired in 1963, and in 1971 was one of only ten players named to the NBA's silver anniversary team. Bob coached for three years, first at Boston College and then for the Kansas City-Omaha Kings. Currently he is a commentator for televised Celtics games.

Sports creates a bond between contemporaries that lasts a lifetime. It also gives your life structure, discipline and a genuine, sincere, pure fulfillment that few other areas of endeavor provide.

BOB COUSY

Sports creates a bond between contemporaries that lasts
a lifetime. It also gives your life structure, discipline and
a genuine, sincere, pure fulfillment that few other areas of
endeavor provide.

Bob Cousy

LAWRENCE LEMIEUX

One of the greatest moments in Olympic history was in the 1988 Olympic sailing competition. Lawrence Lemieux was participating in the fifth race in a seven-event competition when the usual fifteen-knot winds escalated to thirty-five knots. About halfway through his race, holding on to his second-place position, he spotted two sailors, unable to right their boat, being thrown into the waves; only one was visible. After rescuing him, Lemieux saw the second sailor quite far from his boat, sailed to the flailing sailor, and dragged him aboard to safety. After transferring the two men to a patrol boat, Lawrence continued with his race, but it was impossible for him to regain his position and he finished twenty-second out of thirty-two boats. Showing that the spirit of the Olympics is as much about good sportsmanship as it is about skill, the International Yacht Racing Union voted unanimously to award Lawrence second place for that race. Lawrence was also awarded a special sportsmanship award by the president of the International Olympic Committee.

If you perform to the best of your ability, you may not always win but you will never lose.

ROBBY NAISH

Robby Naish is recognized as the greatest windsurfer of all time. At thirteen, he won his first world championship, becoming the youngest world champion ever. During the next sixteen years he dominated the sport, competing in over thirty countries and winning another twenty-two world titles. In 1985 he helped found Quicksilver, a worldwide surfing clothing company. Robby is also involved in cutting-edge windsurfing development and in promoting his sail company, Naish Sails Hawaii, and his board company, Mistral.

Strive to be the best you can be . . . focus, watch, listen, and learn. Try never to be satisfied with "good enough" . . . and above all, love what you do—share that passion with others, and always stay humble. Nobody likes a "big head," no matter how good you are.

If you perform to the best of
your ability, you may not always win
but you will never lose.

**ROBBY
NAISH**

Strive to be the best you can be....
focus, watch, listen, and learn. Try
never to be satisfied with "good enough"...
and above all, love what you do - share
that passion with others, and always stay
humble. Nobody likes a "big head", no
matter how good you are.

Robby Naish
US 1111

Stacy Allison's dreams became reality on September 29, 1988, when she summitted Mt. Everest, becoming the first American woman to stand atop the world's highest mountain. Her career as a mountain climber has spanned over twenty years, during which she has scaled some of the world's highest and most dangerous peaks. At the age of twenty-two, Stacy summitted Mt. McKinley and was part of the first successful women's ascent of Ama Dablan, the 22,495-foot peak known as Nepal's Matterhorn. She went on to become the first American woman to reach the top of Pik Communism, at 24,600 feet, the tallest peak in the Russian Pamir range. After ascending Mt. Everest, Stacy led an expedition on K2, considered the most difficult climbing on Earth. Stacy now lives in Oregon and spends much of her time as a motivational speaker.

Excellence begins with personal commitment . . . belief in ourselves, our goals and the reasons for accomplishing those goals.

Mountaineer Lou Whittaker said, "When it comes down to dying, I want to know what it is like to have really lived." For over four decades Lou has lived on the edge, climbing and leading expeditions to many of the world's highest peaks. By the age of eighteen, Lou had climbed all the major peaks of his home state of Washington. At just nineteen, he began leading climbing expeditions. Over the years Lou has climbed the peaks of Alaska including Mt. McKinley; the Himalayas; Kangchenjunga; and the Karakoram, including K2. He led the expedition that made the first American ascent of the north face of Mt. Everest.

The best is barely good enough!

STACY ALLISON

Excellence begins with personal commitment...
Belief in ourselves, our goals and the
reasons for accomplishing those goals.

Stacy C.

LOU WHITTAKER

The Best is barely good enough!

Lou Whittaker

Bruce Jenner, Olympian, businessman, and philanthropist, is often referred to as "the World's Greatest Athlete." Since his spectacular 1976 Olympic performance, Bruce has epitomized not only endurance but also exuberance and compassion, making him one of America's greatest role models. As a champion of the decathlon, a grueling ten-event competition, he has had to hone numerous and varied skills. After committing himself to thousands of hours of training, Bruce was prepared for the most important competition of his life, the 1976 Olympics Games. Appearing in Montreal excited and confident, Bruce pushed himself harder than ever before, and not only won the gold medal but also broke his own world record. Today, Bruce's compassion for others and his commitment to charitable organizations, such as the Special Olympics and the Pediatric AIDS Foundation, and his passion as a motivational speaker, have solidified his role as a modern-day hero.

Each and every one of us has a champion deep down inside of us. It's up to ourselves to bring that champion out. Never ever give up!!

The most important thing
I know is:
     Each and every one of
us has a Champion deep down
inside of us. Its up to
ourselves to bring that Champion
out.   Never ever give up!!

Bruce Jenner

Born to Korean immigrants, Sammy Lee became the first person of color to win the U.S. national diving championship. After graduating from medical school, Sammy reclaimed his national title in the ten-meter platform diving event. At the London Olympic Games in 1948, Sammy became the first Asian American to win the gold medal. He also won a bronze medal in the three-meter springboard event. At the age of thirty-two, at the 1952 Helsinki Games, doctor and champion Sammy Lee again won a gold medal in the ten-meter event, making him the first male diver to win consecutive Olympic golds. The following year Sammy became the first person of color to be awarded the prestigious Sullivan Award for America's outstanding amateur athlete.

"Disgusted but never discouraged" was and is my motto whenever my divers and my performance was less than Olympic standard. When I coached, I attempted to tattoo that motto into the spirit and minds of my divers and by doing so I was able to challenge, needle, and encourage them to be better in their daily workouts today than they were yesterday, and better tomorrow than today. When they did not I would let them know I was disgusted with their level of improvement but never discouraged that they would and could do better!

It is heartbreaking every four years at the Olympic try-outs to see the tears of agony of those who fail to become an Olympian. But I tell them "you have not failed because of your diving, you forced your peers to dive out of their skulls to beat you." Because of you, your Olympic team had to raise their standard of "Citius, Altius, Fortius." From now on—for the rest of your lives, your motto will be "*Disappointed* but not *discouraged* 'cause I became the best that I could possibly be.

SAMMY LEE, M. D., INC.

"Disgusted but never Discouraged" was and
is my motto whenever my divers and my
performance was less than Olympic
standard. When I coached I attempted to
tattoo that motto into the spirit and mind
of my divers and by doing so I was
able to challenge, needle, and encourage them
to be better in their daily workouts today
than they were yesterday, and better
tomorrow than today. When they did not
I would let them know I was disgusted
with their level of involvement but never
discouraged that they would and could
do better!

It is heartbreaking every 4 years at the
Olympic Try out to see the tears of agony of
those who fail to become an Olympian But I
see them. "You have not failed because of your
diving you forced your peers to dive out of
their skin to beat you. Because of you
your Olympic team had to raise their standard
of "Citius, Altius, Foetius".

From now on -- for the rest of your lives
your motto will be "Disappointed but not
Discouraged 'cause I became the best that
I could possibly be.

Sammy Lee m.d.

Known for his outstanding skill as a batter, as a defensive catcher, and as a manager, Baseball Hall of Famer and three-time MVP Yogi Berra is also loved for his down-to-earth frank personality. Yogi joined the New York Yankees in 1946 and three years later became the starting catcher. As a skilled hitter, he hit the first pinch-hit home run in World Series history in 1947. He hit a grand slam home run in the 1956 World Series and was Don Larsen's catcher during that perfect game. During his eighteen seasons with the Yankees, Yogi played in the World Series fourteen times and won ten times and still holds the Series record of seventy-one hits and ten times on a winning team. After retiring, he managed first the Yankees and then the Mets, leading both teams to pennants.

Giving your all, and trying your best, is all anyone can ask of themselves. Remember it's never over. Just get 'em next time.

It was October 8, 1956, Game 5 of the World Series and the Yankees were pitted against their rivals, the Brooklyn Dodgers, for the World Series title. Three days earlier, during Game 2, Don had been pulled from the game by Yankees manager Casey Stengel after he yielded four walks to the Dodgers. But it was almost as if something magical happened that day. Using a new no-windup pitching technique, Don Larsen beautifully pitched the only perfect game in World Series history. When asked why he thought he rather than a more famous or, frankly, a more skilled pitcher was the first to achieve the feat, Don responded with the modesty and humility that fans have always loved, "Goofy things happen." Yogi Berra recalls that famous game in his foreword to Don's book, *The Perfect Yankee*.

Everyone is entitled to a good day, maybe two, but you have to work for that day.

L.T.D. ENTERPRISES
A BERRA FAMILY CORPORATION

Giving your all, and trying your best, is all anyone can ask of themselves. Remember its never over, just get em next time.

Y. Berra

Everyone is entitled to a good day, maybe two but you have to work for that day.

God Bless

Dick Barry

ANITA DEFRANTZ

Anita DeFrantz, Olympic medalist, lawyer, and the first female vice president of the International Olympic Committee, discovered rowing while still in college. Later, at the University of Pennsylvania Law School, she began racing competitively and participated on every national team from 1975 to 1980. She received a bronze medal at the 1976 Montreal Olympics, was a finalist in the world championships five times, and won six national championships. Anita worked as vice president for the Los Angeles Olympic Organizing Committee and is a member of the U.S. Olympic Committee board of directors and vice president of FISA, the international rowing federation. In 1986, she was elected to the International Olympic Committee. In September 1997 she became the IOC's vice president.

Long ago, I learned an important lesson: The more you give, the more you receive! Giving back to sports has rewarded me with a lifetime of wonderful experiences. There is little that is more wonderful than helping others to succeed!

STEVE REDGRAVE

Olympic rower Steve Redgrave is Britain's most successful oarsman and only the fifth Olympian to win gold medals at four successive Olympic Games. Beginning in 1984 at the Los Angeles Games, Steve and his crew won gold in the coxed four event. In 1988 Steve and his partner won the gold in the coxless pair event; in 1992 he took home another gold from Barcelona. His fourth consecutive gold at the 1996 Atlanta Games was also in the coxless pair event. Steve has recently joined the Sports Ambassador Committee, a charitable organization that provides role models to aspiring young athletes.

Some people train to win. I train to eliminate the possibility of defeat. "Consistency of performance is the name of the game."

Long ago, I learned an important lesson: The more you give, the more you receive! Giving back to sports has rewarded me with a lifetime of wonderful experiences. There is little that is more wonderful than helping others to succeed!

Anita L. DeFrantz

STEVEN REDGRAVE MBE

RSE

Some People Train To Win / Train to Eliminate the Possibility of Defeat "consistency of Performance is The Name of the Game"

All the Best

Steve Redgrave

JEFF BLATNICK

In one of the most inspirational moments in Olympic history, Jeff Blatnick, champion wrestler and cancer survivor, tears streaming down his face, fell to his knees and clasped his hands over his head in thanks after his Olympic gold medal victory. Jeff had qualified for the 1980 Olympics but was unable to compete due to the U.S. boycott of the Moscow Games. In 1982, expectations were high for Jeff's upcoming Olympic performance but, tragically, hopes were dashed after doctors diagnosed the athlete with cancer of the lymphatic system. After undergoing radiation treatment and operations to remove his spleen and appendix, the cancer went into remission. Jeff resumed training and won gold at the 1984 Olympic Games, where he became only the second U.S. wrestler ever to win a gold medal. Currently, Jeff works as an expert commentator and as a motivational speaker and also volunteers his time to charitable organizations including several cancer organizations and the Special Olympics.

If you can't see the *way* . . . how can the *way* see you?
Everyone can fantasize what it is like to reach a successful destination. The reality is, can you see the path that leads you there.

BRUCE BAUMGARTNER

Known as the greatest freestyle heavyweight American wrestler in history, Bruce Baumgartner was undefeated by any American wrestler from 1981 to 1998. He has captured thirteen world championship titles, two Olympic golds, and an Olympic silver and bronze. In 1991 Bruce became the head wrestling coach at Edinboro University of Pennsylvania, where he later led his team to many top-ten NCAA championship finishes. At the 1996 Olympic Games, Bruce was the captain of Team USA and flag bearer for the opening ceremonies. After accumulating more world and Olympic medals than any wrestler in history, Bruce was recently elected to the presidency of USA Wrestling, the amateur-wrestling governing body.

All you can ask of yourself is your best. If you do your best, you should be proud of the outcome.

JEFF BLATNICK
Olympic Champion '84
Wrestling Rules

"If you can't see the way....",

how can the way see you ??"

Everyone can fantasize what it is like
to reach a successful destination.
The reality is, can you see the path that
leads you there.

Jeff Blatnick
Greco-Roman Wrestling
Gold '84

All you can ask
of yourself is your
best. If you do your
best, you should be
proud of the outcome.

Bruce Baumgartner

JAMIE KOVEN

World champion rower Jamie Kovan has garnered international attention since his years at Brown University. While in school he was a three-time U.S. collegiate champion, and in 1994, he was part of the eight-man crew that won the world championships. Voted Brown University's Male Athlete of the Year in 1995, Jamie continued to train for the 1996 Olympic Games, where his crew placed fifth in the eight-man heavyweight crew event. In 1997 he was voted the U.S. Rowing Athlete of the Year, and was also the first American in over twenty years to win the men's heavyweight single event at the world championships. In 1998 he traveled to England, where he won the prestigious Diamond Challenge Sculls, the world's oldest rowing title. As reigning world champion, Jamie is training for the 2000 Sydney Olympic Games.

It's important to respect both your teammates and your opponents. Friendships can make a victory last forever.

SILKEN LAUMANN

Perhaps the most impressive performance of the 1992 Olympic Games was Silken Laumann's bronze medal. Just two months earlier Silken had been the favorite to take home the gold. After winning the World Cup, in 1991, she was named Canada's Athlete of the Year. Tragically, in a pre-Olympic race in Germany, a German boat collided with Silken's boat, driving a piece of wood through the young woman's leg. Bones shattered, muscles and ligaments ripped, and Canada's hopes for the 1992 Olympic gold medal were dashed. However, Silken refused to be dissuaded by her doctors' fears. After rigorous rehabilitation and training, Silken competed in the Olympic Games, winning the women's bronze medal in single skulls. She then won the silver medal four years later in the 1996 Olympics in Atlanta.

I don't think in terms of being extraordinary. I've found some things that are important to me and I pour myself into them. Sometimes, something extraordinary results.

BROWN UNIVERSITY

It's important to respect both your
teammates and your opponents. Friendships
can make a victory last forever.

[signature]

I don't think in terms of being extraordinary.
I've found some things that are important to me
and I pour myself into them.
Sometimes, something extraordinary results.

Silken Laumann
Four time Olympian and World Champion

Football coach Lou Holtz's ability to turn a losing team into winners appears almost magical. His head-coaching career began at William and Mary University in 1969, where, despite three consecutive earlier losing seasons, Lou brought his team to the Southern Conference title in 1970. Lou worked his magic at North Carolina State, Arkansas, and Minnesota before he landed at Notre Dame. Although the Fighting Irish had been struggling, Lou revived them and they captured the national championship. He was a vital component in Notre Dame's twenty-three-game winning streak and in their nine straight postseason bowls. Lou now works as a football analyst for CBS and is a highly sought-after motivational speaker. He takes his expertise to still another medium in his book, *Winning Every Day: The Game Plan for Success.*

The answers to these questions will determine your success or failure. 1) Can people trust me to do what's right? 2) Am I committed to doing my best? 3) Do I care about other people and show it? If the answers to these questions are yes, there is no way you can fail.

OTTO GRAHAM, JR.

Otto Graham's athletic prowess and versatility helped him achieve a lifetime of athletic renown. At Northwestern University, Otto was the 1943 Big Ten football and basketball MVP. After college and World War II, Otto joined the Rochester Royals, which went on to win the 1946 National Basketball League championship (the NBL became the NBA the next year). Later that year, Otto retired from basketball to join the fledgling Cleveland Browns. In this inaugural season, the Browns won the league championship with Otto leading the league in passing. Otto was named All-League Quarterback in four AAFC championships, was a four-time NFL All-Pro, two-time league Player of the Year, and is a member of the College Football Hall of Fame and the Pro Football Hall of Fame.

Ask yourself is it right or wrong and act accordingly.

University of Notre Dame

From the desk of ...

The Answer to these questions
will determine your success or failure.
1) Can people trust me to do
what is right? 2) Am I committed
to doing my best? 3) Do I
care about other people and show it?

If the answers to these three
questions are yes, there is no
way you can fail.

Lou Holtz

OTTO GRAHAM

Ask yourself is it right
or wrong and act accordingly

Otto Graham

Kristine Lilly, one of the best women's soccer players in the world, began competing internationally at just sixteen years of age. Later, at the University of North Carolina, Kristine helped her team achieve four consecutive national championships and was twice named the NCAA's Most Valuable Offensive Player. As the public and sponsors embrace women's athletics, Kristine is offered more and more opportunities to succeed as a professional athlete. In 1991, she was a member of the first FIFA Women's World Championships and she competed on the Olympic gold medal–winning U.S. women's national team. Kristine has played in 87 percent of the matches ever played by the U.S. women's national team and has set the world record for the most international appearances by a male or female international soccer player.

Take pride in what you can control. Giving is the one thing you can control, so always give *your* best and you'll never lose!

Always Believe!

Take pride in what you can control. Giving is the one thing you can control, so always give YOUR best and you'll never lose!

Always Believe!

Kristine Lilly

NIKKI STONE

Despite a back injury in 1996, champion skier Nikki Stone has won over a dozen world-class titles in addition to numerous national titles. She has achieved twenty-two top-five World Cup finishes, is a three-time U.S. champion, and was winner of the 1995 overall World Cup title. At the 1998 Winter Olympics she entered the Games with the strongest track record of any American skier. All her training and earlier competition paid off and Nikki won an Olympic gold medal in the aerials skiing competition. Later that year, Nikki again won the World Cup aerials title, her fourth U.S. aerial championship, and won the Overall Freestyle World Cup title.

You should never be afraid of losing because life's hardest lessons can teach you how to WIN!

JONNY MOSELEY

In 1998 Jonny Moseley has not only won the Olympic gold medal in the freestyle men's mogul event, he has also added smiles and youthful enthusiasm to the event. At a time when skiing is being upstaged by younger events like snowboarding, Jonny manages to keep the attention of the fans. His trademark move, the "heli grab," a 360-degree big-air helicopter maneuver in which Moseley grabs one of his skis mid-spin, delighted the fans at Nagano's Olympic Games. Jonny began as an alpine skier but quickly realized his preference for the more flexible freestyle. He has won national junior titles and two overall titles, in 1995 and 1996, at the World Cup skiing championships.

When trying to accomplish your goal, don't think about the "agony of defeat" or the "thrill of victory." These things will come as a result of what you do, and what you do is the *one* thing you *can* control.

NIKKI STONE
Olympic Gold Medalist

You should never be afraid of losing because life's hardest lessons can teach you how to WIN!

Nikki Stone

Jonny Moseley   *Jonny Moseley*

When trying to accomplish your goal, don't think about the "agony of defeat" or the "thrill of victory". These things will come as a result of what you do, and what you do is the <u>one</u> thing you <u>can</u> control.

Jonny Moseley   Jonny "Big Air" Moseley

Growing up on the impoverished Pine Ridge Reservation in South Dakota and orphaned at twelve, champion runner Billy Mills has had many obstacles to overcome. Through running Billy earned an athletic scholarship to the University of Kansas. There, suffering from feelings of alienation and low self-esteem, Billy joined the Marine Corps. He credits the Marine Corps with instilling in him the discipline and feelings of self-worth he needed to succeed. In the 1964 Olympics 10,000-meter event Billy's victory was astonishing, since he had entered as the underdog. He won the gold medal by three yards. He set the Olympic record with a time of 28:24.4–46, an extraordinary time, because he ran the race 46 seconds faster than his previous personal best. Unfortunately, Billy was not able to run the traditional victory lap, because so many runners had fallen so far behind that his victory lap might have interfered with their completion of the race. His moment of glory had passed, but twenty years later, in 1984, he returned to Tokyo to run his victory lap in an empty National Stadium. Billy Mills, the first American to win the gold medal in the 10,000-meter event, was inducted into the U.S. Olympic Hall of Fame in 1984.

The greatest degree of competition is not for me to compete against you or you against me, but for each of us to reach within the depths of our capabilities and to perform to the greatest of our potential.

BILLY MILLS
10K GOLD PROMOTIONS

" The greatest degree of
competition is not for me to
compete against you or you
against me, but for each of us
to reach within the depths
of our capabilities and to
perform to the greatest of
our potential. "

Billy Mills
Olympic 10k Gold

Born in 1946, Bela Karolyi trained in the track-and-field event of hammer throwing, in his hometown in Transylvania, before turning to gymnastics coaching in college. He came onto the international gymnastics scene at the 1976 Montreal Olympic Games with protégée Nadia Comaneci. Her perfect ten scores launched her career and the Bela Karolyi coaching legend. After defecting to the United States in 1981, Bela moved to Houston, Texas, to run a gymnastics school. Bela's rigorous tutelage has produced twenty-seven Olympians, seven Olympic champions, fifteen world champions, and twelve European medalists. His gymnasts have won the U.S. National All-Around title eight times. Bela has coached many of women's gymnastics' most famous athletes, including Comaneci, Mary Lou Retton, Dominique Moceanu, and Kerri Strug. The world will never forget Bela, carrying his protégée, injured and weeping Kerri Strug, to the platform to receive her gold medal at the 1996 Olympics. Working at Karolyi's World of Gymnastics, Bela and his wife, Martha, train six hundred gymnasts a year.

I believe in human decency, and I believe in good time and fun offered by sports, but most of all I believe in playing with your heart, with every fiber of your body, fairly, squarely, by the rules—but *to win*. And I believe that any man's finest moment is that when he has worked his heart out in a good cause and lies exhausted on the floor but *victorious*.

I believe in human decency, and I believe in Good Time and Fun offered by sports, but most of all I believe in playing with your heart, with every fiber of your body, fairly, squarely by the rules — but TO WIN.

And I believe that any man finest moment is that when hi has worked his heart out in a good cause — and lies exhausted on the floor — but — VICTORIOUS.

Bela Karolyi

Arguably one of America's most popular athletes, gymnast Mary Lou Retton catapulted to fame in 1984 when she became the first American woman ever to win an Olympic gold medal in gymnastics. Mary Lou's unusually solid and strong body helped her dominate the vault event and the floor event, while her rapport with the audience and her wide smile secured her a place in Americans hearts. In the 1984 Games Mary Lou also won two silver medals for team and vault, two bronze medals for uneven bars and floor, and the all-around gold medal in women's gymnastics. With a total of five Olympic medals, Mary Lou has one of the best records in American Olympic history. Awarded numerous titles in 1984, including *Sports Illustrated*'s Sportswoman of the Year, the Associated Press Female Athlete of the Year, and the Women's Sports Foundation Athlete of the Year, Mary Lou retired from competition in 1986.

The key to success is positivity, excellence, possessing great expectations, and seizing the moment. All this would be impossible without faith in God. It is *He* who supplies you with the strength, desire, and courage to make the most of your talents. I'd like to share a quote that I've always admired: "To know greatness and to keep humility."

MLR
ENTERTAINMENT, INC.

The key to success is positivity, excellence, possessing great expectations, and seizing the moment. All this would be impossible without faith in God. It is HE who supplies you with the strength, desire, and courage to make the most of your talents.

I'd like to share a quote that I've always admired:
"To know Greatness
and
To Keep Humility"

Mary Lou Retton

Ralph Boston, internationally ranked track-and-field high jumper, member of the National Track and Field Hall of Fame, and a member of the Olympic Hall of Fame, competed for over a decade, during which time he broke several world records, including that of track star Jesse Owens. In 1959, Ralph Boston ranked fourth in the country as a high jumper. On August 12, 1960, at the Olympic trials, Ralph stunned the international track-and-field community by not only setting a world record of 26 feet 11¼ inches in the long jump but also by breaking Owens's twenty-five-year record in the process. Just a few weeks later, Ralph broke Owens's twenty-four-year Olympic record with a jump of 26 feet 7¾ inches and took home the long jump gold medal. Less than a year later, in 1961, he broke his own world record by jumping 27 feet ½ inch. He is the first person ever to surpass 27 feet. He defended his world record through 1965, when he set his last world record at 27 feet 5 inches. Ralph competed for eight more years, receiving a silver medal at the 1964 Olympics and a bronze in 1968. After retiring in 1969 he worked as a commentator at track-and-field events and in the administration of the University of Tennessee.

Practice does not make perfect! Only perfect practice makes perfect. Once you have begun to practice perfection, you are on your way to achieving *Excellence!* When you reach that plateau, there is no greater feeling in the world.

Practice does NOT make Perfect.'
Only Perfect Practice makes perfect.
ONCE you have begun To practice
Perfection, you are on your way
To achieving Excellence! When you
reach That Plateau, There is NO
greater feeling in The World.

Ralph Boston

'60 '64 '68

Bill Koch, graduate of MIT and of the Harvard Business School, internationally ranked yachtsman, anticrime activist, and founder of the Oxbow Group, one of the largest privately held companies in America, has been honored by a wide variety of organizations. In 1990 and 1991, Bill won the Maxi Yacht World Championships and went on, in 1992, to be the winning skipper of the America's Cup. In addition, he made history when he launched the first all-women America's Cup team, acting as their CEO. He is a member of the America's Cup Hall of Fame, was voted Yachtsman of the Year by *Yachting* magazine, and given the Advanced Women's Leadership Award from the Women's International Center and the First Women's Choice Award from Miracle House. In 1993, Bill started the William I. Koch Crime Commission on Crime Reduction and Prevention. His commission brings members of communities from his native Kansas together with national experts on crime prevention in order to find creative solutions to fight crime.

Almost all of our limitations are self-imposed. Those that are not can be overcome by cooperation with others whose strengths complement our weakness. Therefore, with the right attitude, the right focus, and the right dedication, ordinary people can accomplish extraordinary things.

Almost all of our limitations are self imposed. Those that are not can be overcome by cooperation with others whose strengths compliment our weakness.

Therefore, with the right attitude, the right focus, and the right dedication. ordinary people can accomplish extraordinary things.

Bill Koch
Skipper of America³, USA-23
Winner of the 1992 America's Cup.

Named after a town in Idaho, downhill and slalom skier Picabo Street has always been unique. A fun-loving nonconformist, Picabo showed a natural talent for skiing early on and was named to the U.S. ski team at the tender age of sixteen. However, frustrated with Picabo's lack of motivation and discipline, her coaches kicked her off the team in 1989. Realizing that she had to make some changes, Picabo started training with a newfound determination. In 1991, she was invited back onto the team. After winning a silver medal in the downhill event at the world championships and another silver at the World Cup races, she was anxious for the 1994 Olympics. Her hard work paid off and Picabo won an Olympic silver medal in the downhill event and went on to win a gold medal in the Super G at the 1998 Olympics in Nagano, Japan.

Follow your dreams as long as you live! Never be afraid to go out on the limb to live up to *your* expectations. Always do things your way and Have Fun!

PICABO STREET

Follow your dreams as long as you live! Never be afraid to go out on the limb to live up to <u>your</u> expectations. Always do things your way and Have Fun!

Picabo Street

TOM WHITTAKER

Professor of adventure education and wilderness leadership at Prescott College in Arizona, Tom Whittaker teaches his students about the benefits of wilderness training and about the enviornment. Tom, mountaineer, author, teacher, and motivational speaker, was struck by a car in 1979, resulting in the loss of his right leg. Two years later, overcoming depression and anger, he founded the Cooperative Wilderness Handicapped Outdoor Group. In May 1998, along with members of CWHOG and four Sherpas, Tom accomplished a long-sought-after goal. He summitted Mt. Everest and became the first disabled climber to stand on top of the highest mountain in the world. He describes mountain climbing this way: Assaulted by the elements in rarefied air, mountaineers do battle with the giants of geography. In wind and snow, on rock and ice they toil upwards. It has no intrinsic purpose; it is of no earthly good. There is no one to watch, no adoring public, no accolades. Financially it is often ruinous. Why then do we do it?

The spirit of mountaineering is the need to sustain the soul through adventure. It is not the summit, it is the journey to the summit that is the essence of what we do. The outer journey leads us within. The rewards are in self-knowledge that comes from pursuing your dreams in wild places, with love and courage.

BRADFORD WASHBURN

World-class mountaineer, explorer, and cartographer Dr. Bradford Washburn has been gathering and contributing a vast array of knowledge to the fields of exploration and science. Over half a century ago he was the first to use high-frequency radios for field communication. After World War II, he worked in collaboration with the U.S. Army developing cold-climate and high-altitude equipment. Dr. Washburn was also instrumental in the development of the first precise large-scale map of Mt. Everest.

The wisest advice that anybody ever gave was what Goethe said at the turn of the century: If there is something that you *think* you can do—Or even *dream* that you can—*begin it*!! Boldness has *mystery* and *power* and *magic* in it!

The spirit of mountaineering is the need to sustain the soul through adventure.

It is not the summit, it is the journey to the summit that is the essence of what we do.

The outer journey leads us within. The rewards are in self knowledge that comes from pursuing your dreams in wild places, with love and courage.

Tom Whittaker.
Summit May 27th 1998.

the wisest advice that anybody ever gave was what Goethe said at the turn of the century:

If there is something that you THINK you can do or even DREAM that you can —

BEGIN IT !!

Boldness has Mystery
and Power
and Magic in it!

Sincerely yours —

Bradford Washburn

Red Auerbach was the winningest coach in NBA history with 958 wins. Born in Brooklyn, New York, basketball coach Arnold "Red" Auerbach's small stature does not affect his reputation as one of the most revered coaches in basketball history. In 1946 Red coached the Washington Capitols of the new Basketball Association of America to 123 victories. However, he is best known for his success with the Boston Celtics. Under Red's guidance the Celtics won nine NBA championships. He retired as coach in 1966 but stayed on with the Celtics first as general manager until 1984. During his eighteen years as general manager, the Celtics won sixteen NBA titles. Retiring as GM in 1984, Red became president of the Boston Celtics. He is a member of the Basketball Hall of Fame.

To be a successful coach you should be and look prepared. You must be a man of integrity. Never break your word. Don't have two sets of standards. Remember you don't handle players—you handle pets. You *deal* with players. Stand up for your players. Show them you care—on and off the court. Very important— it's not "how" or "what" you say but what they absorb.

Celtics ♣

ARNOLD "RED" AUERBACH
Vice - Chairman

To be a successful coach you should be and look prepared. You must be a man of integrity. – Never break your word. –

Don't have two sets of standards. – Remember you don't handle players – You handle pets. – You *deal* with players. –

Stand up for your players – Show them you care – on & off the court.

Very important – it's not "how" or "what" you say but what they absorb

Red Auerbach.

Journalism has been a part of Bob Costas's life since he broadcast as a student over Syracuse University's radio station. His career has spanned over twenty years and numerous professional sporting events, including several Olympic Games. Broadcasting for football, baseball, and basketball, Bob has covered five NBA championship series, five World Series, and six Super Bowls. Bob's enthusiasm and knowledge have helped him become one of America's best-loved sports broadcasters. Throughout his career he has been honored with twelve Emmy Awards and named National Sportscaster of the Year seven times.

The best thing about sports is the sense of community and shared emotion it can create. And one of the worst things about sports is the irrationality that those same emotions can produce.

Expertly using every conceivable medium, Bud Greenspan is one of the leading sports historians in the world, and is renowned for his *16 Days of Glory* Olympic film. Bud has produced a series of films, books, and magazine articles that document some of the greatest moments in Olympic history. Among other accomplishments, Bud has produced a television series titled *The Olympiad*, numerous documentaries, and a highly acclaimed NBC television movie about Olympic athlete Wilma Rudolph. Throughout his career, Bud has won seven Emmy Awards, a Lifetime Achievement Award from the Directors Guild of America, a Peabody, and the prestigious Olympic Order, by President Juan Antonio Samaranch and the International Olympic Committee in 1985.

Never look to the ground for your next step. Greatness belongs to those who look to the horizon.

Bob Costas

The best thing about sports is the sense of community and shared emotion it can create. And one of the worst things about sports is the irrationality that those same emotions can produce.

Bob Costas

Cappy
Productions Inc.

NEVER LOOK TO THE GROUND
FOR YOUR NEXT STEP
GREATNESS BELONGS TO THOSE
WHO LOOK TO THE HORIZON.

Bud Greenspan

Steve Scott's career in track and field has spanned over a decade during which he has achieved national and world-class status. While attending the University of California Irvine, Steve won three consecutive NCAA championships in the 1,500-meter event. He is a six-time winner of the national outdoor championships in the 1,500-meter. Although he finished first at the 1980 Olympic trials, he did not compete due to the U.S. boycott of the Moscow Games. However, at the World Championship Games Steve won a silver medal in his 1,500-meter event. Steve is one of only two runners in history to have run the mile in less than four minutes over one hundred times. On July 7, 1982, he set the current American record for the fastest mile at a time of 3:47.69. Steve presently lives in California, where he manages a running camp, does promotional work, and is a television commentator for ESPN. His book, *Steve Scott the Miler: America's Legendary Runner Talks About His Triumphs and Trials*, tells his inspiring story.

The real heroes in this world are not the richest, most popular, or most visible, but those people who give of themselves to help others without asking or expecting anything in return.

The real heros in this world
are not the richest, most popular, or most
visible, but those people who give of
themselves to help others without asking
or expecting anything in return.

Steve Scott
80-84-88 Olympian

Dennis Conner is most famous as the four-time winner of the America's Cup, more than any other skipper in the history of the Cup. He is an Olympic yachtsman, four-time United States Yachtsman of the Year, author, and accomplished artist. Since 1851, when this international yachting event began, America had always competed and won the America's Cup trophy. Trying to defend an American winning streak of 132 years, the longest record in the history of sports, Dennis was defeated by the Australian crew in 1983. Dennis did not accept defeat easily and returned, under immense pressure, to compete in 1987—and regained the cup. A year later he again sailed to victory, skippering another winning boat in the America's Cup races. His career wins include the Star Class World Championship in 1971 and 1977, two Congressional Cups, and in 1976 an Olympic bronze medal. Currently, Dennis is training for America's Cup 2000 and is a leader in numerous charitable endeavors.

Excellence implies more than just being good . . . it implies a striving for the highest possible standards!

DENNIS CONNER SPORTS, INC.

Excellence implies more than
just being good ... it implies
A striving for the highest
possible standards !

Dennis Conner

JESSE ANNA LANTERMAN

Rhode Island resident and Special Olympics athlete Jesse Lanterman has been competing nationally for half her life. A high school senior, she has won numerous gold, silver, and bronze medals. Her main event is swimming, in which she specializes in the backstroke, freestyle, and breaststroke. She has also successfully competed in bowling, basketball, and golf. After graduation from high school Jesse plans to continue participating in the Special Olympics and supporting her fellow athletes.

Do my best winning medals.

PAULA NEWBY-FRASER

Ironically, no one has won more Ironman Triathlon World Championships than Paula "Ironwoman" Newby-Fraser. Born in 1962, in Harare, Zimbabwe, Paula was admittedly overweight and not athletic while she was in college. After graduating, Paula took up running to get in shape. In January 1985, her impulsive decision to enter a short-course triathlon event resulted in victory. Despite having done little training, Paula not only won the race but set a new course record. The prize included a trip to Hawaii to compete in the annual Ironman Triathlon, considered the premier event of its kind. Paula began to train and race rigorously. She won the event in 1986, and for the next nine years Paula dominated the women's Hawaiian triathlon, finishing in first place eight times and breaking records in the bike course and the marathon. In 1990, she was voted the Women's Foundation's Professional Athlete of the Year and became a spokeswoman for women's fitness. Paula is a member of the Ironman Hall of Fame.

Handle your life right now, because that's all there is! You won't get to the finish line until you deal with the ground right under your feet!

Do My Best Winning Medals

Jesse Lanterman

Paula Newby-Fraser

Handle your life right now, because
thats all there is! to won't get
to the finish line until you
deal with the ground right under
your feet!!

Paula Newby-Fraser

After two heartbreaking near misses at Olympic gold medals in 1988 and 1992, speed skater Dan Jansen had a tremendously supportive crowd rooting for him at the 1994 Winter Olympics. In 1988, just a few hours before he was to compete, Dan learned that his sister had died of leukemia. Although he had been the favorite to win both the 500- and the 1,000-meter races, Dan, obviously upset, fell during both his races. Then, in 1992, he missed winning a bronze medal in the 500 by just 0.16 of a second. At the 1994 Games in Norway, Americans and Norwegians alike cheered Dan on. Finally, in the 1,000-meter race, Dan won a gold medal and set a new world record.

Set your goals high, never set limits. Give 100% of yourself to achieve those goals. If you can look back and know you've given 100%, then you have succeeded!

Dan Jansen
Speedskater • Olympic Gold Medalist 1994

Set your goals high, never set limits.
Give 100% of yourself to achieve those
goals. If you can look back and know
you've given 100%, then you have succeeded!

Dan Jansen

Member of the National Horse Racing Hall of Fame, Chris McCarron began racing at the age of nineteen and never dreamed that his tremendous racing skill would keep him competing for the next twenty years. Since 1974, Chris has won over 6,240 races, been named ESPN's Outstanding Jockey of the Year, and became the first jockey to win the Breeder's Cup Classic twice. With career earnings over $167 million, Chris ranks second in all-time jockey earnings. Despite his dizzying schedule, Chris donates time and money to the charity he cofounded for disabled riders. He has also provided horse-racing analysis and commentary for NBC television.

"Luck is when preparation meets opportunity." My goal every day is to go out and create some luck.

— Chris McCarron —

"LUCK IS WHEN PREPARATION MEETS OPPORTUNITY"

My goal every day is to go out and create some luck.

Chris McCarron

Olin Stephens, a legend in the sailing world, has designed and raced a multitude of champion racing boats including seven America's Cup winners. After attending the Massachusetts Institute of Technology, Olin began participating in many races, including the America's Cup race in 1937, the last America's Cup featuring the 130-foot "J" boats. His love of sailing and his expert engineering knowledge helped him design *Finisterre*, three-time winner of the Bermuda Race, as well as *Columbia, Constellation, Intrepid,* and *Courageous*, winners of the America's Cup races. In 1970 Olin was honored with the "Master Designer" award from *Product Engineering* magazine and received an honorary award from Stevens Institute of Technology.

Experience leads me to believe that luck has been the most important element in my participation in sports. Not only has good luck been important in the outcome but recognition of luck's place in all competition has helped me hold a course between hubris and discouragement.

Olin J. Stephens II

Experience leads me to believe that luck has
been the most important element in my participation
in sports. Not only has good luck been important
in the outcome but recognition of luck's place in
in all competition has helped me hold a course
between hubris and discouragement —

Olin Stephens

S ince it was thought to be too strenuous for women, there was no female Olympic marathon event until 1984. Proving that she possessed not only grit and strength but also tremendous perseverance, Joan Benoit Samuelson, in August 1984, won the first-ever Olympic women's marathon. In 1979, after entering and winning her first Boston Marathon, Joan underwent surgery on both Achilles tendons. Despite having to take time off from training, she won her second Boston Marathon in 1983 and broke the world record by almost three minutes. With her sights set on the 1984 Olympic trials, Joan trained constantly to prepare. But just two weeks before the trials she suffered excruciating pain in her right knee. Barely able to walk, Joan opted to undergo arthroscopic surgery. After the surgery, the pain was gone but she still had to rest her leg in addition to having postoperative leg treatments. Determined, Joan decided to try to compete, and only seventeen days after the surgery, she placed first in the trials. A little over two months later, Joan won the first-ever Olympic women's marathon, proving that nothing was too strenuous for her.

Whatever the pace, wherever you go, follow your heart and your soles will follow.

Whatever the pace, wherever you go,
follow your heart and your soul will follow.

Jo Beaf Samuelson

On December 26, 1983, at the age of twenty-one, Art Berg broke his neck in a serious automobile accident, leaving him a quadriplegic with only partial use of his arms and hands. However, the tragedy did not thwart Art's accomplishments, nor did it dampen his infectious upbeat attitude. Since the accident he has won three national sales awards, been named the Young Entrepreneur of the Year by the Small Business Administration, and written two bestselling books, *Some Miracles Take Time* and *Finding Peace in Troubled Waters*. He is a world-class wheelchair athlete who enjoys many sports, including skiing, rugby, and parasailing. On July 10, 1993, he set a world record by becoming the first quadriplegic, at his level of ability, to race more than 100 miles by completing an ultra marathon of 325 miles between Salt Lake City and St. George, Utah. He is a member of the National Speakers Association and is widely sought for his inspirational message.

I do not believe in failure—only results! If I can change what I do, I can always get a different result. Some of the greatest miracles of my life have not come about by grand events—but rather by the little things I have chosen to do . . . every day.

I do not believe in failure —
only results! If I can change
what I do, I can always get a
different result. Some of the
greatest miracles of my life
have not come about by grand
events — but rather by the
little things I have chosen to
do ... everyday.

Known as "the Rocket" because of his powerful fastball, Roger Clemens has been one of the most formidable pitchers in the major leagues for over fifteen years. He joined the Boston Red Sox as a first-round draft pick in 1983. Within a year he had won the first of his five Cy Young Awards, set a major league record by striking out twenty players in a nine-inning game against the Mariners, and been named the Red Sox co-Rookie of the Year and the league MVP of the season. Playing with the Red Sox for over a decade, Roger beat every team at least once and led the majors with 197 wins and 2,682 strike-outs. In 1996, he signed with the Toronto Blue Jays and set Blue Jay records for the most strikeouts in a game and in a season. Three years later he was traded to the World Champion Yankees. Throughout his career he has been named an American League all-star seven times and pitcher of the month thirteen times. He holds the record for most strikeouts in a single game and is tied for both the most wins and the most shutouts in Red Sox history. When he's not breaking American League pitching records, Roger works with a charitable organization he established in 1992, the Roger Clemens Foundation.

*They call me lucky when *preparation* and *opportunity* come together. That is all the luck you need! Take advantage of it!!!

* THEY CALL ME LUCKY
WHEN PREPARATION AND OPPORTUNITY
COME TOGETHER. THAT IS ALL THE LUCK
YOU NEED! TAKE ADVANTAGE OF IT!!!
"ROCKET"

Florence Griffith Joyner, the talented, beautiful, and refreshingly flamboyant track-and-field star, was known as the "world's fastest woman" or simply as "Flo Jo." Attending college at California State University and then at UCLA, Florence was a two-time NCAA sprinting champion. She competed in the 1984 Olympic Games but was discouraged by her second-place standing. Plagued by self-doubt, she quit running and worked as a hairstylist. But after urging from her soon-to-be husband and coach, Al Joyner, Florence decided to give competitive running another try. Appearing at the 1988 Olympics with flowing long hair, polka-dotted two-inch fingernails, and hot pink tights, Flo Jo wowed the judges and audience with her amazing speed and endeared them to her with her vivacious personality. Upon winning three gold medals and one silver medal, Flo Jo the celebrity was born. She retired from running in 1989 and focused on endorsement work, designing her own line of sportswear and on developing her own fitness video. Several years later she was elected to the Track and Field Hall of Fame. Her untimely death due to a heart condition, at just thirty-eight, shocked and saddened the world, though her spirit will live with generations to come.

"I cried every day for a new pair of shoes until I saw the man with no feet." My daddy told me this most inspiring thought one day and ever since, I have lived my life according to what it means to me. There have been times when I thought I was having troubles and being the only one depressed, but every time I read or say that thought, my problems disappear instantly. I have shared it with family and friends hoping that it would inspire them as well, and it has. It's a picker-upper for me! Just knowing that someone out there in life has it more difficult than I, helps me appreciate life to its fullest. And when I see someone sad and feeling down, I share that thought with them and the results are always uplifting for me.

"I cried everyday for a new pair of shoes until I saw the man with no feet"

My daddy told me this most inspiring thought one day and ever since, I have lived my life according to what it means to me. There have been times when I thought I was having troubles and being the only one depressed, but every time I read or say that thought, my problems disappear instantly. I have shared it with family and friends hoping that it would inspire them as well, and it has. It's a picker-upper for me! Just knowing that someone out there in life has it more difficult than I, helps me appreciate life to its fullest. And when I see someone sad and feeling down, I share that thought with them, and the results are always uplifting for me.

Florence Griffith Joyner
"Flo Jo"

Flo Jo.

Basketball star Wilt Chamberlain is arguably the best scorer in the history of basketball. At 7 feet 1 inch, Wilt dominated the court not only in shooting but also in assists and rebounds. After attending the University of Kansas, where he was named National College Basketball Player of the Year, Wilt went on to play with the Harlem Globetrotters. In 1959, he joined the NBA's Philadelphia Warriors, with whom he averaged a whopping 37.6 points a game in his rookie year. By his third year, scoring 4,029 points, Will became the only player ever to exceed 4,000 points in a single season. He averaged 50.4 points, another new NBA record, and had the most time on the court of any other player at an average of 48.5 minutes playing time per game. During this amazing season, Wilt scored 100 points in a single game, a feat yet unmatched. A member of two NBA championship teams, the first player to score more than 30,000 points, and the first player to lead the NBA in shooting seven consecutive times, Wilt Chamberlain set new standards of excellence for the sport of basketball.

I've played many games, but I have never played any game just to pass or fill time, because time is far too important to play games with.

I've played many games,
but I have never played any
game just to pass or fill
time; Because time is too
too important to play
games with.

Wilt
Chamberlain

Mark McGwire hit his first home run at his first Little League at-bat as a ten-year-old. Although he was recruited to be a pitcher at the University of Southern California, midway through his college career he switched from pitcher to first base to add some power to the lineup. In 1984, Mark won a gold medal as a member of the United States Olympic baseball team. Mark was named the American League Rookie of the Year in 1987, when he hit .289 with 49 home runs and 131 runs batted in.

In 1988, Mark won his first American League pennant while a member of the Oakland A's and was still with the A's in 1989 when they won their second consecutive pennant and went on to beat the San Francisco Giants in the famous "earthquake" World Series.

In 1997, after being traded to the St. Louis Cardinals, Mark became the first player other than Babe Ruth to smash fifty or more home runs in consecutive seasons. In 1998, he did it for a third consecutive season when he hit seventy home runs to break the single-season home run record of sixty-one held by Roger Maris since 1961.

In August 1997, Mark founded the Mark McGwire Foundation for Children and will donate $1 million a year for three years to it. The foundation was established to offer funding support to organizations that have a successful track record in improving the lives of mentally and physically abused children.

Never make the same mistake *once*!!

NEVER MAKE THE SAME
MISTAKE ONCE!!

70 HRS 98

MARK McGWIRE

He's still the most recognizable man on earth, and thirty-eight years after he burst upon the scene as a gold medal winner at the 1960 Rome Olympics, Muhammad Ali remains a revered figure, known and loved throughout the world. Ali brought unparalleled speed and grace to his sport while his charm and wit changed forever what we expect a champion to be. His accomplishments in the ring were legendary—two fights with Sonny Liston, where he proclaimed himself "the Greatest" and proved he was; three epic wars with Joe Frazier; the stunning victory over George Foreman in Zaire; and dethroning Leon Spinks to become heavyweight champion for an unprecedented third time. But there was always far more to Muhammad Ali than what took place in a boxing ring. Ali's life and career have been played out as much on the front page as on the sports page. His early embrace of the Nation of Islam and his insistence on being called Muhammad Ali instead of his "slave name," Cassius Clay, heralded a new era in black pride.

Today, championing the causes of the developing world has become a major focus of Muhammad's life. Through Global Village and other philanthropic groups, Muhammad has been instrumental in providing over twenty-two million meals to the world's hungry. Of all his charitable activities, Ali derives his greatest joy from working with children, in such organizations as the Make-A-Wish Foundation and the Special Olympics' organization Best Buddies and Herbert E. Birch Services. For his tremendous humanitarian efforts, Muhammad has been the recipient of countless honors and awards, most recently the Messenger of Peace honor, presented by United Nations Secretary General Kofi Annan.

The most important thing I know about the spirit of sport is that one has to be fit in both body and mind. Whether it's boxing, basketball, or badminton, one must be ready to succeed before entering the arena . . . long before the lights come up.

G·◇·A·T

GREATEST OF ALL TIME, INC.

1998

The most important thing I know about the spirit of sport is that one has
to be fit in both body and mind. Whether it's boxing, basketball, or
badminton, one must be ready to succeed before entering the arena... long
before the lights come up.

Muhammad Ali
98